"*The White Allies Handbook* is a great lesson,
more important than ever."
—**Rosanna Arquette**

"*The White Allies Handbook* is a book written with such
practical, intentional, and community-informed guidance
for its readers. It's a work which provides those seeking
to be allies to racial justice movement work led by Black
and Brown people with opportunities to engage in sincere
reflection and introspection. Sometimes, all we need
is to take a figurative first step; Lecia Michelle's book
provides the path. Highly recommended."
—**McKensie Mack**

THE
WHITE
ALLIES
HANDBOOK

4 WEEKS to Join the
Racial Justice Fight for
Black Women

Lecia Michelle

www.kensingtonbooks.com

DAFINA BOOKS are published by

Kensington Publishing Corp.
119 West 40th Street
New York, NY 10018

All Kensington Titles, Imprints, and Distributed Lines are available at special quantity discounts for bulk purchases for sales promotions, premiums, fund-raising, and educational or institutional use. Special book excerpts or customized printings can also be created to fit specific needs. For details, write or phone the office of the Kensington special sales manager: Kensington Publishing Corp119 West 40th Street, New York, NY 10018, attn: Special Sales Department, Phone: 1-800-221-2647.

The DAFINA logo is a trademark of Kensington Publishing Corp.

Library of Congress Card Catalogue Number: 2022934639

ISBN: 978-1-4967-3837-0
First Kensington Hardcover Edition: August 2022

ISBN-13: 978-1-4967-3839-4 (ebook)

10 9 8 7 6 5 4 3 2 1

Printed in the United States of America

For my sister, Joya.
I miss you every day.

CONTENTS

INTRODUCTION

B efore you begin your journey, I want to dispel some misconceptions about what it actually means to be an ally. As you make your way through this book, you'll see I repeatedly say allyship means "action." Having a Black Lives Matter yard sign or including a hashtag on your social media account that says #BelieveBlackWomen doesn't make you an ally. These are just a few examples of passive decisions white people make to convince themselves they're allies without doing any actual anti-racist work to fight racism. It makes them feel good, and too often those feelings mean more to them than stepping outside of their comfort zone to directly confront racism. When white people make passive decisions about how to address racism instead of ones that drive real change, they're telling me that they're unwilling to step outside of the comfort of their whiteness to fight for my equality. A small, ineffective gesture is the totality of their brand of allyship. It will never be enough to challenge the status quo and push our equality to the forefront. It's whiteness at work, and it's rampant in this country.

We only have to look at American politics to see how entrenched white supremacy and racism are in the United States. The 2020 presidential election is over, and President

Joe Biden and Vice President Kamala Harris now lead our nation. Four years of tyranny are over. Or are they?

Fifty-five percent of white female voters cast their ballots for Donald Trump. That's up from 53% in the 2016 election. Nearly seventy-four million Americans voted to reelect a man who praised white supremacists and called protestors thugs. They supported a leader who tried to abolish President Obama's Affordable Care Act, even as many of them took advantage of that health coverage. They cast a ballot for a president who never spoke out against police brutality, even after the horrific videotaped death of George Floyd at the hands of Minneapolis police. They said yes to a president who knew months earlier how deadly COVID-19 could be to our nation and purposely downplayed it. They proudly voted for a man who watched as hundreds of thousands of American citizens died from the virus—many of them Black. After all that, his supporters still wanted him to remain in the Oval Office for another four years. His racism and white supremacy didn't deter them. If anything, it spurred them in greater numbers to come out and vote. It also drove thousands of them on January 6, 2021, to attack the Capitol in an effort to help Donald Trump remain in office, even though he lost the election. These people would have murdered members of Congress had they been able to find them that day. Instead, they turned their anger on law enforcement, and many of those who defended the Capitol that day will never be the same. That's where we stand as a nation. This blatant support of racism should be the tipping point for self-described allies. Even if they didn't vote for hatred, they know people who did exactly that.

In the midst of all this upheaval, Black people still fight for equal voting rights—a right that white people in this country take for granted. Countless times, I've worked with white people who challenged me when I say that slavery didn't end so much as it evolved. Freed slaves weren't allowed to vote. They couldn't just live anywhere they wanted. Many rented land from white people and worked as sharecroppers. They toiled away for little pay since everything they needed to farm, they purchased on credit. They also lived under the constant threat of violence by the Ku Klux Klan.

As a Black woman, I can't stress enough the importance of having white people as allies. So it's important you understand what that word means. "Ally" is a title we give white people when we see you using your privilege to actively fight racism. Don't assume you're an ally. The white people I consider allies have done the hard work of confronting racists, even when it's people they love. They understand and expect the discomfort that comes with having those difficult conversations. They've dedicated themselves to becoming effective allies. No amount of reading Black history or quoting Black people brings you any closer to that title. Allyship isn't theoretical. It requires action. While I do want you to read and study about Black people, I also want you to understand that standing up in the face of racism, both explicit and implicit, is what's required of allies.

Time and again, white people make lackluster attempts at being allies by participating in marches and quoting passages from books. The turnout for the Women's March was impressive. However, how many white women did any actual ally work once they hung up their pink pussy hats? Now is the time for white people to fully commit themselves to supporting us. That means recognizing their own racism and abolishing it. That also means standing up to racists—especially family and friends. Allyship means fighting against hatred everywhere. That's how we will have any chance of defeating racism in this country. Yes, we voted, and a new administration now sits in the White House, one committed to fighting systemic racism. We also must do our part. The fight against racism isn't won or lost through policy. It's defeated by talking to the very people who protect and support it. White people must initiate those hard conversations with the goal of changing minds or making it impossible for those racists to spew hatred around them without any consequences.

I created **The White Allies Handbook** with the unique purpose of giving white people actionable directions they can follow on their way to becoming allies to Black women. While books like Robin DiAngelo's *White Fragility: Why It's So Hard for White People to Talk about Racism* explain why white people are uncomfortable discussing race, they don't provide a clear way to help them break through that barrier. This handbook shows you how to conquer the discomfort and why it's crucial that you succeed. Allyship is a journey, and no matter where you are on that path, this book provides information that will help you become more effective allies. Allyship means you listen to Black women.

You believe our stories. You support us anywhere you can. You find opportunities to amplify our voices. You create avenues for our successes. You don't allow white supremacy and white privilege to insinuate their way into any spaces where their presence prevents Black women from receiving an equal chance to excel in life.

During the 2016 election, I was searching for a space that supported Hillary Clinton. Like many people, I found the Facebook group Pantsuit Nation. I wanted a community where women like me could talk about all the possibilities for us if this country elected a female president. At the time, the group had close to four million people. Most of the posts shared in the group were from people talking about their own personal experiences. However, I noticed that when Black women posted anything remotely related to racism, white members shouted them down. They didn't want to hear it. They only wanted positive stories. They called the Black women divisive and racist. Other Black women, including myself, tried to tell these white people that they were the ones perpetuating racism through their actions. We explained how Black women overwhelmingly supported the Democratic ticket, and it was time the party took our concerns seriously. It fell on deaf ears. Not only did the white members attack us, we received no support from the group's moderators and administrators. The turning point for me was when a Black woman posted a topic specific to the experiences of Black women and asked that only we respond. White members caused an uproar, and the administrators handled the situation poorly. Not only was the original poster harmed by the vitriol, but many Black women who came to her defense also were harmed. I decided right then that I would start my own Facebook group, a safe space for women of color and a place where white people could learn how to become allies. In December 2016, I created "Real Talk: WOC & Allies for Racial Justice and Anti-Oppression." Since then, we've mentored over 1,100 white women on allyship and provided a safe haven for thousands of women of color. The mentoring program gave me the idea to create a resource for white people.

THE WHITE ALLIES HANDBOOK provides potential allies with clear, concise information they can use to effectively fight racism with Black women. The market is inundated with books explaining racism and the need for white people to step up and help fight it, but the authors don't show readers how to begin. My handbook gives you a self-directed path to becoming an effective ally. The book is written so potential allies can kick-start their journey in four weeks. That means every day you should be working through this handbook and thinking about allyship. It's also important to document the journey, so you'll need a journal on hand before you begin. In addition to answering questions and completing actions, you'll use your journal to write down any challenges and address any feelings of defensiveness or anger.

Throughout the book, you'll be given prompts about the materials. These prompts—in boldface and italicized so they stand out—urge you to stop and think about the information and how you would react in certain situations. Each chapter introduces a new concept followed by discussion questions and action items you must complete in order to confront your own racist beliefs.

It's also imperative to find another white person as an accountability partner so you can support each other and work through obstacles together. You'll hold each other accountable to do the work and continue the process.

I also don't want you to burden or harm Black women with questions about any information or homework from the book. You shouldn't seek us out for assurances that you're doing the work correctly. That communication stays within your accountability relationship or with white members of any anti-racist groups you join.

Learning to become an ally takes deep processing on your part. So don't rush through this book. Otherwise, you won't have time to really digest the information. **THE WHITE ALLIES HANDBOOK** is a practical guide that you can revisit and come away each time with new knowledge about yourself and racial justice work. I suggest purchasing (or borrowing from your local library) at least one other book about racism while you work through this handbook. I created a list of recommended books in the "Further Reading" section of this handbook. You can also choose your own book.

Take advantage of your local library and its collection. Ask the librarian for suggestions about what you can read or watch. You also can search YouTube for documentaries, lectures, and films. Take the time to visit a museum or attend a lecture. Many college campuses have free events. Once you join an anti-racist group, you'll gather information from other allies and Black women (I'll talk more about joining a group later). The point is that you keep learning. If you want to educate others, you need a variety of resources you can recommend to them. Remember to use your journal to write down your thoughts and ask questions you want to explore later.

The questions and actions at the end of each chapter will challenge you, and it will be easier to complete them with another white person who is also reading this handbook to begin their ally journey. If you can't find someone in real life, reach out through social media. You can have more than one accountability partner and join more than one affinity group. Make sure you're open to sharing your journals with each other and talking through your defensiveness. Remember that defensiveness and anger are just ways to deflect from your feelings of discomfort.

Even though ally work is difficult, it will never be harder than enduring racism and living under the cloud of oppression. So when you feel this work is too much for you, remember you have the privilege to stop and go back to your comfortable life where you only think about yourself and your own needs. We don't have the privilege of disappearing into whiteness. We're stuck with white people and your insistence on telling us who we should be and how we should behave. Retreating because someone hurt your feelings is a lazy excuse for your unwillingness to change. In order to support me and other Black people, you must acknowledge and fight against your own racism. Your current mindset won't cut it. You've had your entire life to cultivate whiteness, and now I'm telling you to think in a different way. You can't always believe what you see in the media or what your family tells you about us. You've internalized those lessons. Now you must exorcise them.

As you progress through this book, keep in mind that allyship is a lifetime commitment. My goal is to introduce you to tools you'll need to join the anti-racism fight and continue that fight for the rest of your life.

Part I

LISTENING AND LEARNING

Week 1

Chapter 1

STARTING YOUR ALLY JOURNEY

Recognizing and unlearning your racism

Welcome to the first step in your (most likely long and difficult) journey. However, if you commit yourself to this process, you'll learn to become an effective ally. My goal is for you to be more than just "not racist." I want you to become *anti*-racist, someone who can no longer stand on the sidelines. Instead, you're compelled to occupy the front lines alongside me in this fight. Have your journal handy so you can write down any thoughts or questions you may have. *Are you apprehensive? Excited? Take a few minutes to take a personal inventory of your feelings.*

You're not ready to stand by my side just yet. First, you must educate yourself about racism before you take a position on the front lines. Don't jump right into the work of fighting racism. I've had white women actually attempt to lead racial justice groups within months of starting their journey as an ally. This mistake ends up causing us more harm than good. That's because they rush into every situation, bringing along their white supremacist views and racist ideology. You can't fight racism if you don't really understand that part of the fight is within *yourself.* It doesn't make sense to start doing the work without understanding that you're perpetuating racism *and* you've harmed Black women. That's why it's important to take the time to understand what it means to be an ally.

"Ally" is a title we give you when we see you actively fighting against racism. Don't call yourself an ally until *we* say you're one. I've met white people who can quote every well-known book on racial justice and are well-versed in Black history. That doesn't mean I can trust them. This work includes more than just reading books about racism. Allyship means action. **What are some ways allies can take action against racism?** We'll also discuss this later in the book. Remember, allyship requires doing the work necessary to help us fight for our freedom. Anything short of that means you're just a spectator—a lurker.

A few years ago, my "Real Talk" moderators noticed most of the white women in the group weren't posting or commenting. This silence was unacceptable, so I decided to require that white women actively participate in the group. They needed to post and comment so they could learn. Taking part in conversations around race teaches allies the valuable lesson of how to support Black women without taking up too much space. Knowing when your voice is so loud that it drowns out ours is an important lesson in allyship. We call this centering yourself. **Why do you think centering prevents you from becoming an effective ally?**

The purpose of "Real Talk" wasn't simply to provide reading materials to potential allies. These white women needed to actually engage with each other and with women of color in the group so they became accustomed to the discomfort of discussing subjects like racism, white supremacy, and white privilege. Even with my new rule, white women still wouldn't initiate or engage in any discussions. So I directed my moderators to remove any white women who hadn't commented in the last three months—700 in total.

I wanted to push the remaining white women into understanding that silence should never be the default option when learning to become an ally. "Real Talk" provided them with a space to ask all their questions. It also taught them not to burden Black women with the harmful task of educating them. Although administrators and moderators—many of whom were women of color—did step in to educate when necessary, white women learned to ask other white allies to help them work through many of their questions. This allowed more seasoned allies to draw on their own personal experiences and teach newer allies.

As part of your education, I want you to understand the history of racism in this country so you can more effectively educate other white people. I'm not asking you to take a college course or get a degree. You don't have to be an expert. You should, however, have a solid background on what racism is and how it affects every aspect of Black lives. Really take in that history even if it makes you uncomfortable. For example, we're taught that President Lincoln freed the slaves in 1863 by signing the Emancipation Proclamation. Yet these freed Black people continued to work on the same plantations under the same conditions for generations. They still picked cotton from sunup to sundown. They still faced the same violent overseers. Black people couldn't just up and leave. Where would they go? We received only partial truths about slavery in school. *Why was this history left out of our education? How do you feel knowing you weren't taught enough about Black history?*

There's a reason why we're taught so little about racism in school. It's by design. If you downplay the history, then obviously Black people are exaggerating the seriousness of it, right? The education you received in school convinced you that slavery ended long ago, and now Black people need only work hard to succeed. It's as simple as that. I grew up learning almost nothing about Black history. I learned about Harriet Tubman and Dr. Martin Luther King, Jr., but nothing about Shirley Chisholm, Fannie Lou Hamer, or Ida B. Wells. Years later, I sought out that education on my own. So many Black women shaped this country. Yet their accomplishments are rarely acknowledged in classroom curriculum. That's why it's important that allies know the accomplishments and sacrifices of Black women in a country that continues to marginalize us. *Take some time now to read about the three aforementioned women. What stood out to you about them? Why do you think you never learned about these Black women in school?*

I didn't realize my own ignorance until years later, and I'm still discovering stories I didn't know. I can trace my family back eight generations in this country, and yet that history abruptly stops with my enslaved ancestors. Black people helped build this country. It's our blood, sweat, and tears that allowed white people to amass fortunes they still pass down from generation to generation. On the other hand, we have nothing to show for our painful past other than a lost ancestry and continued oppression. Yet we're the very ones to whom white people say, "Pull yourself up by your bootstraps." Once you read about the history of racism in this country and its lasting effects on housing, education, health care, politics, etc., you'll understand how little hard work has to do with white people succeeding and Black people struggling.

In 2020, the American Heart Association released a call to action focusing on the relationship between structural racism and health care disparities. The article states: "Structural racism inequitably limits opportunities for social, economic, and financial advancement, which in turn results in a complex interplay among race, social determinants, and health that has negative consequences." In other words, many Black people are prevented, through racist laws and policies, from attaining the same goals as white people. The article also explains that, even if Black people achieve the same socioeconomic status as white people, health care disparities still persist. Earning a degree also doesn't mean we will be treated equally. Throughout their careers, college-educated Black people are more likely to face unemployment and earn less than their white counterparts. In addition, racism affects the health of Black people. We experience mental health issues such as depression and stress that, in turn, affect our physical health. Black people are more likely to be essential workers, which means during the COVID-19 pandemic, we were more likely to be exposed to the virus. Structural racism also prevents us from accessing quality health care. That means we have higher instances of preexisting conditions—one of the reasons Black people died of the virus at higher numbers.[1]

That's why I want you to learn about the history of racism in this country and really think about the lives of Black people. Compare our lives to your own. When you take a walk in your neighborhood, consider what could happen if I were strolling through that same neighborhood and you or one of your neighbors called the police because you didn't think I belonged there. You can't ever put yourself in our shoes, but be honest about the reasons you or your neighbor would make that call. We've seen it play out numerous times, sometimes with deadly consequences. If you can begin to understand the violence of your actions, it will help you when you actually start your anti-racist work. You can convey to other white people that their motives are based on their racism and that racism might kill us. You'll begin to recognize when a situation could lead to violence if you or another white person make a decision based on your racist beliefs. You'll know to intercede when these situations arise.

A good understanding of racism also helps you converse

1   Churchwell, K., Elkind, M. S. V., Benjamin, R. M., Regina M., Carson, A. P., Chang, E. K., Lawrence, W., Mills, A., Odom, T. M., Rodriguez, C. J., Rodriguez, F., Sanchez, E., Sharrief, A. Z., Sims, M. & Williams, O. (2020). Call to action: Structural racism as a fundamental driver of health disparities: A presidential advisory from the American Heart Association. *Circulation, 142,* e454–e468. http://doi.org/10.1161/CIR.0000000000000936

with other white people. Without this knowledge, you won't know how to respond to many of the arguments you'll encounter from white people who make excuses for racism.

Have you used any of the following responses?

- *You insist that reverse racism is real: Reverse racism is a myth. Black people can't be racist. Racism includes the added characteristic of power. White people have the power to influence housing, education, quality of health care, etc. Black people do not.*

- *You say talking about race is divisive and actually makes the problem worse: White people have been mostly silent on the prevalence of race in this country. Yet it's not getting better.*

- *You ask why everything has to be about race: Race is a social construct created by white people to seat themselves firmly on top. That's why it's up to you to defeat the institution white people created and many of you still fight to uphold.*

An important aspect of this work is learning about the insidious nature of racism. Simply put, it's everywhere. **What do you think racism means?** Let's clarify its definition. *Racism* doesn't mean one person hating another person because of her race. That's *prejudice* or *bias*. You'll have other white people challenging you on what exactly racism means. What you need to understand is that racism encompasses a power dynamic that white people possess and that most minorities do not. Subsequently, Merriam-Webster changed its definition of racism to:

> *a belief that race is the primary determinant of*
> *human traits and capacities and that racial differences*
> *produce an inherent superiority of a particular race.*
>
> *a: doctrine or political program based on the*
> *   assumption of racism and designed to execute its*
> *   principles*
>
> *b: a political or social system founded on racism,*
> *   racial prejudice or discrimination*

This new definition includes its systemic nature. That means the racist systems in place create inequities—specifically for Black, Hispanic, and Indigenous people—in health care, education, housing, criminal justice, employment, politics, etc. **Using these categories, think of some ways racism affects Black people.** It's easy for white people to deny that there are inequalities because you choose to ignore them or make excuses as to why you consistently come out on top. Anyone can find statistics supporting health care disparities. For example, Black women are two to three times more likely to die from pregnancy-related complications than white women.[2] Black women get breast cancer at the same rate as white women. Yet their death rate is 40% higher.[3]

---

2   Beim, P. (2020, June 6). The disparities in healthcare for Black Women. Endometriosis Foundation of America. https://www.endofound.org/the-disparities-in-healthcare-for-black-women

3   Richardson, L. C., Henley, S. J., Miller, J. W., Massetti, G. &

Many Black women, including my sister, have stories of visiting a doctor, only for their concerns to be dismissed or downplayed. Since her early teens, my sister suffered from cysts in her breasts. Over the years, she had dozens removed. The doctor told her that because of these cysts, she was at a higher risk of developing breast cancer. When she began getting mammograms, she also received sonograms to make sure there was no breast cancer. She was vigilant for twenty-five years. She never missed a mammogram. One day she called me to say her breast didn't feel right. She got a mammogram to see what was going on, but they didn't find anything out of the ordinary. They told her she was fine. But she knew something wasn't right. I suggested a second opinion. A few weeks later, she got another mammogram. The results showed she had Stage-4 breast cancer, and the cancer had spread to her eye. We were devastated. The doctor said it was a slow-growing cancer that probably had been there for years. The other facility missed the growth more than once. In other words, her cancer should have been caught much earlier. My sister went through chemotherapy, changed her eating habits, and fought as hard as she could. Two years later, I sat at her hospital bedside holding her hand as she died.

Let's talk education inequality. Did you know that schools in Black and Brown communities receive less funding and support than schools in white communities? In fact, nonwhite school districts receive a whopping $23 billion dollars less

---

Thomas, C. C. (2016). Patterns and trends in age-specific Black-white differences in breast cancer incidence and mortality - United States 1999–2014. *Morbidity and Mortality Weekly Report, 65*(40), 1093–1098. http://dx.doi.org/10.15585/mmwr.mm6540a1

than white school districts.[4] *How do you think Black parents feel sending their children to schools that are underfunded and underperforming?* Visit any major corporation and see the paucity of diversity in its ranks and the ocean of whiteness at the executive levels. Mercer's *When Women Thrive: 2020 Global Report* surveyed over 1,500 organizations with a total of 7 million employees. It found that white men made up 85% of executive positions.[5] When you hear white people argue that other races simply refuse to work hard enough to succeed, don't believe it. The more you read and work with other allies, the better tools you'll possess to counter that argument with facts strongly supporting the story of a country that continues to systematically oppress many of its citizens simply because of the color of their skin.

Understanding and undoing your biases is a lifetime process. That's a hard pill to swallow—that you perpetuate racism and white supremacy. I want to challenge your idea of what it means to be racist. Racists aren't just members of the Ku Klux Klan, the Alt-Right, or white people videotaped verbally or physically assaulting Black people. These people are obvious in their hatred, and anyone can see them for what they are. However, they're far outnumbered by what I call "casual racists."

---

4   EdBuild. (2016). Current funding systems are outdated, arbitrary and segregated. *EdBuild*. Retrieved November 26, 2020, from https://edbuild.org/content

5   Mercer. (2020) Let's get real about equality. When women thrive: 2020 Global Report. *Mercer*. Retrieved November 27, 2020, from https://www.mercer.com/content/dam/mercer/attachments/ private/gl-2020-wwt-global-research-report-2020.pdf

If you already feel defensive right now, push through it and keep reading.

Racism has little to do with whether you're nice. Nice white people can be just as racist as anyone else. I've encountered them, and they're not rare by any stretch. My junior year of college, I worked as a resident assistant. One day, a girl who lived on my floor knocked on my door. Like me, Desiree was from a small town. I understood how intimidating going away to college could be. So it wasn't unusual that she sought me out. I invited her in and we sat down. We chatted about her classes for a while and then about our respective towns. It was an uneventful conversation until this:

> DESIREE: *I'm so glad you're my R.A. You're not like other Black people.*
>
> ME: *What does that mean?*
>
> DESIREE: *You're not a nigger.*

I was furious but not surprised. I told her that calling Black people *niggers* was disgusting and hurtful. I said I don't have friends who use that word. She tried to tell me she didn't mean anything by it, but the damage was done. I would be her R.A. but our friendship was over. You might believe that Black people don't regularly hear white people saying *nigger*, but I can assure you we each have a story, and many of those stories occurred recently. I also want you to understand that racism doesn't belong to any one political party. It doesn't matter if you're a Democrat or a Republican. Many white people have fallen into the trap that "liberal" means not racist. You probably

23

ask yourself how it's even possible for you to be racist when you support causes that benefit people like me. It's great that you support us through your votes, but in your day-to-day lives, how are you fighting racism?

Actually, I should ask how you're harming us. If you believe that your liberal politics prevent you from being racist, you're oppressing us without even thinking about it. That's unacceptable when you're talking about doing the work of being anti-racist and an ally. If you're only voting but refuse to speak up when you see racism, you must understand the consequences of your inactions and why you cannot stay silent. I learned the hard way that white liberals harm us, too. Before I knew better, I believed I only needed to be wary of white conservatives who support an agenda steeped in white supremacy. However, I've worked alongside white liberals, and I've rarely seen any speak up about racism or any other injustices in the workplace. **Do you think liberal or progressive white people can be racists?**

Years ago, I worked at a large financial institution. I was in my early thirties and by then adept at spotting racists. This place was no different. Within a week, a white man made himself known. "Allen" rarely spoke to me. It was obvious through his actions he disliked me and didn't want me on his team. Although he said nothing directly to me, he spread plenty of lies behind my back. It shouldn't surprise you that my career ended before it even began. Although this man had a reputation as a bully, the white people in the office either took his side or ignored the situation altogether. I became an office pariah. I couldn't do anything right. My manager at the time, a gay white man, refused to step in and ultimately blackballed me even further. That's because I wouldn't stay silent and just do my job like he demanded. I spoke up against this bully's harassment, but it didn't matter. I left that position under a cloud of negativity and the hard lesson that I couldn't depend on white people—even self-described white liberals—to do the right thing.

I've lost count of how many times I've been on the receiving end of such racism, and not one white person stepped in to support me. That's how I learned white people will protect themselves and each other, rarely willing to personally risk anything—even when the Black person is someone they consider a friend. It was a hard lesson. If there were more allies in these spaces, white people wouldn't have endless opportunities to oppress us.

Think about how you view Black people. **Do you make excuses as to why we're treated differently than you?** Consider the times you've asked yourself what we did to deserve such treatment. Be honest here. I want you to remember why you thought something negative about us simply because of our skin color. Think about how you perceived our behavior compared to the behavior of a white person doing exactly the same thing. Really dig deep into why you react more favorably toward other white people.

This is just one example of a larger problem. You refuse to allow us the same level of autonomy you enjoy. No one is policing your body. No one is dictating your life. No one is questioning your decisions.

Yet that's exactly how Black people exist in a racist, white supremacist society.

REINFORCE YOUR KNOWLEDGE

Use your journal to answer the following questions and discuss how you completed the actions.

Scenario

You're in a school board meeting. The board has decided to make the celebration of Black History Month optional for students. There are no Black board members, but you notice there are Black parents in the audience. A Black woman stands up and says, "I disagree with this decision. My child learns white history all year. Why can't white children learn Black history for a month?" A white male board member responses, "We're not banning it. We're just not making it a requirement." You stand up to speak in support of having Black History Month required for all students. What do you say?

Question 1: Find an accountability partner. This can be in person or online. Lay down the ground rules about how you'll keep each other on track. How often will you talk? Share your journals with each other. Be open with your questions. Anytime you feel defensive or angry, work through that with her.

Question 2: Write down a time you exhibited racism toward a Black woman. Who was it? Why did you do it? Thinking back, how do you think she felt about your actions?

Question 3: What do you already know you need to address about yourself with regard to racism and why?

Question 4: How/where did you first learn about racism?

Question 5: When was the last time you saw someone else

saying or doing something racist? Did you speak up? If not, what would you do differently next time?

Question 6: Consider the following questions and write a short paragraph about your thoughts:

- *Do you worry about encountering doctors who, because of your skin color, refuse to take your health concerns seriously?*

- *Do you worry about your children attending the substandard school in your community, or pin your hopes on them winning a lottery to attend a better school in a different (white) neighborhood?*

- *Do you assume you can move into any neighborhood you choose without its residents attempting to force you out?*

Action

Start building your personal library of anti-racism resources. Include this handbook, any resources from the list of "Further Reading" at the back of this book, and the other book on racism you're currently reading. Find a mix of resources such as articles, videos, blogs, etc. Ask other allies for recommendations. This information will be invaluable to pass on to other white people when you're trying to educate them.

Chapter 2

UPLIFT OUR VOICES

Following the leadership of Black women

White allies work on addressing their racism and are willing to take a stand to fight for the rights of Black people. They possess a deep understanding of both racism and white privilege because they know this knowledge helps them become effective allies. In 2020, researchers saw that most studies used only self-described allies. Subsequently, they decided to delve deeper into the characteristics of allies chosen by people of color compared to those of self-described allies. The first study compared the qualities of white allies who were nominated by people of color to white allies who were not nominated (also called self-described allies) by people of color. The second study compared two groups: allies whom people of color were confident would speak up for them if they witnessed racism and friends whose response to racism they were uncertain of. Some of the categories researchers examined included low prejudice, internal motivation to respond without prejudice, and acknowledgment of privilege.

In both studies, allies nominated by people of color

showed awareness of privilege and a willingness to take action to fight for the group to which they were allied. These allies also viewed this group positively and wanted to stand up for the issues important to them. In Study 1—comparing allies nominated by people of color to self-described allies— nominated allies rated themselves higher in their attitudes toward people of color. They also scored themselves higher on their motivation to take action. They rated themselves much lower than non-nominated allies in the anti-people of color scale. *What is the problem with calling yourself an ally versus earning the title by having a person of color call you one? How could this prevent you from growing as an ally?*

The takeaway from this portion of the study for white people should be this: Calling yourself an ally means nothing if you're unwilling to address your racism and take action when needed to fight for us. People we describe as allies already do this work. We give them the "ally" title because we can count on them to stay motivated to dismantle racism. They respect us and see us as equals. They listen and learn.

Study 2 compared allies nominated by people of color to friends nominated by people of color. In this case, allies were those that people of color were certain would stand up with them against racism. Friends were people they weren't sure would do this. Results found that allies again rated themselves higher than friends in regard to their positive attitude about people of color. They also scored themselves higher in motivation and activism and lower on the anti-people of color scale. Friends didn't score themselves as low as you might think on these scales. The results show that, while not nominated as allies by people of color, they see themselves as people who would stand up for people of color; don't have anti-people of color attitudes; and are motivated to respond without prejudice.[6] White people oftentimes see themselves as defenders of racism without ever having done anything to illustrate that. That's why I felt an urgent need to create a space to show them how to do real ally work. I founded "Real Talk: WOC and Allies for Racial Justice and Anti-Oppression" in December 2016 and created a strong group of Black female administrators who assist in running the group and calling in white women when they cause harm. I have a diverse group of moderators who also address problems in the group and bring them to the attention of myself and the other administrators. We're the checks and balances needed for the work to succeed. We decide the group's direction, mission, and goals. The white women moderators, trainers, and mentors also give us valuable feedback from other white women in the group. It works because our main goal is always to support women of color. *How will you feel as a member of a group focusing on advocating for Black women? What will you do if you feel uncomfortable?*

I wanted "Real Talk" to provide a safe space for women of color while also training white women to become allies. My goals for the group haven't changed since its inception. We need more allies—a lot more allies. We provide a two-week

---

6   Ostrove, J. M. & Brown, K. T. (2018). Are allies who we think they are?: A comparative analysis. *Journal of Applied Social Psychology,* *48*(4), 195–204.

training that new white members must complete before joining the group. The training and mentoring are led by a white woman who has created curriculum and anti-racism training for decades. It was a natural fit for her to lead this training and oversee what we call the "Mending Room." This is a place where white women who misstep learn about their harmful behavior and receive guidance on preventing it in the future. It's not a fun place to visit, but the lessons are given fairly and firmly. *How does the idea of addressing your harm with other allies make you feel? Why is it important that you do so? What is your responsibility as the person who missteps?*

The training gives potential members an introduction to racial justice work. This introduction also protects the women of color in the group. Otherwise, we would encounter new white women who recklessly enter "Real Talk" without considering how their words and actions affect other group members. That's not to say we don't have white women enter the space and exhibit racism. We do. Other white women in the group call them out. They then take them into a different online space to help them figure out where they went wrong. Once they understand their misstep, they craft an apology to post in the main area that is addressed to whomever they harmed. It has taken us years to get to a place where the group relatively runs smoothly and where I feel confident that, when a white woman hurts a woman of color, we address it swiftly and effectively. I depend on the white women in the group to take on this duty. It isn't the job of any woman of color to address these issues. However, if we do decide to educate you, show your appreciation by listening to what we say and learning from it. *Why are white people solely responsible for addressing the harm other white people cause? How could it negatively affect women of color in the group if they took on the task of working with white people who exhibit racism?*

As an anti-racism leader, I can tell you firsthand that white people who have friends that are people of color often inflate their willingness to address racism. They believe that their close relationships with us make them less likely to be perpetrators of racism. They believe that, since that one Black person likes them, they must be doing something right. White people with Black spouses or children are some of the most dangerous white people I've ever encountered. They refuse to believe they even have the capacity for racism because of their relationship. It would be easy to blame the Black person in their lives. However, it's the responsibility of white people to educate themselves about white supremacy and the role they play in protecting it instead of using Black people as shields for their own racist behavior. I've encountered numerous white women in "Real Talk" who have used their relationships with Black people to explain why they're already allies. However, allyship is a difficult journey that requires constant self-reflection about your actions and the motives behind those actions. It takes much more than a relationship with a Black person for white people even to come close to understanding the challenges we face in this country. The idea that they have less work to do than anyone else is patently false and dangerous to Black women.

While they may have relationships with Black people, these relationships don't make them less likely to exhibit racism and white supremacy. In fact, it rarely means they're anti-racist at all. *What harm do white people cause when they use Black people as shields to defend their racism?*

White people start anti-racism groups even when they don't have the tools to effectively lead them. Many label themselves as allies without actually doing any real anti-racism work. They inflate their allyship to convince themselves and others that they're ready to lead other white people who want to become allies. These white people believe that they've learned enough to now guide others when, in reality, they've barely addressed what it means to actually be an ally. They certainly haven't done the inner work to acknowledge their own racism. This inflated belief of their own ally worth doesn't come with any concrete skillset or knowledge; it comes with the idea that allyship can be quickly learned and taught. The problem with this line of thinking is that learning how to be an ally requires **unlearning** much of what you thought you knew. If your idea of being an ally means you read some articles or watched a documentary, you're not an ally and you have no business leading other white people. In fact, you'll convince other white people that this work is easy and it only takes a short period of time before you're ready to help lead this movement.

A study conducted on a white anti-racist organization illustrates how white people can work in racial justice spaces while also holding themselves accountable. The organization, active in community organizing, touted strong leadership and checked in with an outside, Black-led organization to hold themselves accountable for doing the work. The research for this article focused on what the group learned over the past year as they attempted to cut the county sheriff's budget to impact racist politicians and police. Participants were put into two focus groups and given a questionnaire and survey related to their perception of how the group performed over the past year. The findings showed that the members understood that even the smallest tasks were essential to a strategy succeeding. These seemingly insignificant accomplishments led to major changes. Participants also discussed the importance of being adaptable as situations change. They explained how their organization would pivot when necessary in response to new challenges.

The responses highlighted the importance of growth and learning through actually doing the work needed to achieve your goal. This included talking to stakeholders as well as learning how to organize fundraising events. Participants understood the importance of developing relationships and forming connections. One member explained it as people coming from dissimilar backgrounds for a common goal. Another described it as supporting one another through the process. They understood the importance of strong leadership and planning. Participants said the group was well-organized and they could depend on their leaders to uphold the principles of the group. Another participant said their presence at the public hearing and the reduction of the budget proved effective leadership and organization.[7]

The aforementioned illustrates the commitment needed to lead an anti-racism group and the importance of having a Black-led organization that will hold you accountable for completing your mission. Most white people who want to lead don't know what leadership focused on anti-racism and allyship should look like. It's more than creating the group and sitting back while people have discussions. Ask any "Real Talk" member who joined even a year ago, and they will tell you about battles in the main area—which we call the "Living Room"—where white women have doubled and even tripled down when they're called out because of their racism. The white women who help educate others must regularly address their own harmful whiteness and convey those lessons in this space.

That's hard work.

Think about it. Not only are they working through another white person's racist violence, they're simultaneously checking their own potential to harm in the process. These allies understand the ease of slipping back into the comfort of whiteness by excusing racism or questioning whether the occurrence was even racism to begin with. It took us two years to hone the process of holding white women accountable for their harm in a way that addresses the harm and allows them to learn from it. Why so long? Because it takes

---

7   Diebold, J. (2021). "We're going to show up": Examining the work of a white anti-racist organization. *Journal of Community Practice*, *(29)*1, 11–22. https://doi.org/10.1080/10705422.2021.1881936

at least that long for white people teaching other white people to work through their urge to defend each other, not succumb to white fragility, and—most importantly—maintain their commitment to uplift and protect women of color in the group. *Why would white people gravitate toward a racial justice group led by other white people? What lessons would they fail to learn in these white-led spaces?*

Leading racial justice groups while also acknowledging and addressing your own racism doesn't work. Your job should be first and foremost to educate, but how can you do that while also running the day-to-day administrative duties for the group? What happens when you misstep? Who calls you in to address your harm? I doubt you'll even be open to working through it. That's because whiteness is much more alluring than protecting us. It feels safer and easier. White people defend it with their lives. It takes a long time to recognize the violence of this behavior. Therefore, if white people lead an anti-racist group, this is the majority of the work—educating other white people about their white fragility, white supremacy, and white privilege. If you have no Black women leading or advising that space, how do you know you're really addressing the core issues surrounding racism?

And this is only the beginning of effective anti-racism leadership. Most white people can't even get past this stage; so how would white people who want to lead groups work through these challenges so they don't harm the very people they claim to want to protect? Constantly acknowledging their own capacity to harm is also a large part of anti-racism work. How can white people successfully do this work if they've convinced themselves they're better allies than other white people? That's a dangerous mindset, believing you've reached a level of allyship where you'll never again harm us. There is no place for it in anti-racism work. The stakes are too high, and Black women don't want allies who refuse to work on themselves and their potential to do us harm. *What are the consequences to Black women when white people believe they've learned enough about being allies? Why do white people believe they have nothing more to learn?*

It's whiteness at work when any white person new to anti-racism work believes they have learned enough to teach others. That's like saying you read a few medical books and you're now qualified to perform open-heart surgery. Let me be clear on something. I'm not worried about the white people. Most will fail miserably in these spaces. I worry for the women of color who will be hurt through their neglect and incompetence.

From the outside, leading an anti-racism group probably looks glamorous, but I can tell you firsthand that it isn't. When done right, you'll have *some* success stories—but many more failures. Unfortunately, most white people will stop doing the work because it's too hard to set aside their white supremacist beliefs and white privilege. That doesn't mean these people will stop running racial justice groups. They simply won't address the violent racism happening in those spaces. It's easier to ignore it and hope it goes away. That's why it's so important you join groups with Black women leading them. *What will you do as an ally when you see racism that is unaddressed in a racial justice group?*

Accountability can't happen when white people lead racial justice groups without Black women at least advising them. It's impossible to effectively guide discussions related to white supremacy and white privilege if Black women aren't involved to weigh in with their own experiences of racism and how they've been affected by it. White people must continually educate themselves. However, if they only surround themselves with other white people, they create an echo chamber where no one is held accountable for harm and no real progress is happening. *How do white people break out of their comfort zones when learning to become an effective ally?* Without Black women challenging whiteness and confronting the inevitable racism that arises within racial justice groups, white people will believe they're working toward becoming an ally. In reality, they're prioritizing their own comfort by allowing other white people to excuse their behavior. Held unchecked, white people will downplay racism by saying their intentions were good or they couldn't possibly be racist because someone close to them is Black. Black women know this line of reasoning is dangerous to us. Potential allies should never put their feelings above their ally work. *How does downplaying harm affect white people learning how to be an ally? What are some ways they can get back on track?*

Black women like me provide you with leadership, education, and awareness of racial justice and what you can do to fight with us. The resources are endless, and many of them are free for you to use so you can continue to learn as an ally. That's why you should never demand that we educate you on any topic related to our experiences about racism. Yes, many of us are in the trenches doing the work of dismantling it, but respect those of us who don't want to expend the energy of handholding you while you argue with us about our lived experiences and whether you, in fact, have white privilege. These topics aren't harmless debates. They're painful to discuss and even worse when a white person disbelieves or challenges us on topics in which they have no firsthand experience. So when a Black woman says she won't educate you about racism, respect that and look for answers on your own. You can use this book, the references at the end, and other allies in your racial justice group. Take the time to find the information without demanding that a Black woman provide those answers. Not all of us want to teach you. Too many of us have been burned by white people who say they want to learn, only to gaslight us into a painful debate where they attempt to downplay or erase what we've experienced.

It's important that you find a diverse community or organization led by Black women. Listen to different Black voices and draw your knowledge from all those experiences. Never assume that one Black woman speaks for all of us. The beauty of Black women is that every one of us is different. Don't dismiss our experiences because you disagree or think we're exaggerating. You're not the expert on racism and white supremacy. We are. Your job is to learn from us. Get in the habit of listening more and talking less so you begin to understand the challenges we face and how we handle a racist society that tries to define us in ways we would never define ourselves. Black women are the experts on how and when we've experienced racism. So if you're too busy talking and defending yourself, you'll miss any lessons you could have learned to become a better ally. *Why is it important that allies listen more than they talk? What are some ways to get into this habit?*

Black women lead the charge for racial justice in many arenas. In the 2020 presidential and senatorial elections, Stacey Abrams and LaTosha Brown spearheaded initiatives to educate Black voters and get them to the polls. Those endeavors drew thousands of volunteers from all walks of life to ensure that Black votes were counted. The diversity of people who helped was amazing, and they succeeded. Assisting organizations tasked with ensuring fairness and equality is an important part of ally work.

Black people will continue to face voting challenges for the foreseeable future until there are checks and balances in place to ensure we have an obstacle-free path to exercise our right to participate in elections. If you're looking for ways to support voting rights, search Facebook for groups that are addressing this issue and join a few. Why Facebook? Most organizations have a Facebook page where they define their work and allow you to join. Depending on your interest, there will be a group addressing that topic. If you're interested in health care reform, housing, education, politics—really anything—join a Facebook group so you can help find solutions to the systemic racism Black women face. *What are some interests you have relating to racial justice, and why are you interested in them? What do you currently know about those topics?*

Between your racial justice group and your group addressing specific issues, you should get plenty of resources and ways to progress as an ally. Racial justice groups cover a variety of topics while also providing information you can use to further your own education. Read that information and revisit it when you need clarification. Add it to your own library so you can pass that information on to other potential allies. *Why is it important to constantly read about racism instead of depending on the same resources?* These online spaces are also a great way to find other white people on the path to becoming an ally and who, like you, want to learn more about how they can support Black women. Many members of "Real Talk" have met in person, attended marches, and formed affinity groups. They use these connections to discuss their challenges and ask questions about allyship. *How do you feel about connecting with other allies? How will this benefit your work as an ally?*

Once you join a group, remember your purpose is to educate yourself, not burden Black women with traumatic, invasive questions. You never want to add to our pain by demanding we educate you. Plenty of us educate through writing and speaking. Seek out these resources instead of assuming we want to relive trauma just so you can learn. Your membership in a racial justice group doesn't center your feelings about racism. It doesn't center you at all. *How will you work on not centering yourself in these racial justice spaces and as an ally in general?* The work should always focus on Black women and how you can better support us. Becoming an ally *is* important, but it should never come at a cost of harming Black women as you educate yourself. That's a lesson you'll learn once you participate in discussions about racism. You'll make mistakes. That's all part of your education.

Black women and more experienced allies will tell you when you've caused harm. Your response will determine whether you move forward from your mistake. You must come to the conclusion that anger and shame won't kill you, but your racism and white supremacy might kill *us*. Learn to work through these emotions so you can get to the root of the reason why you exhibited racist behavior. **How will you work to prevent your emotions from hindering your allyship? What does that work look like?** Excuses will never fly in these groups, but potential allies—and even more experienced ones—can fall into the trap of defensiveness and excuses when confronted about their racism. That's not conducive to moving forward. If you're defending your actions, you're not listening when other white people try to explain how you've harmed us.

You have an affinity group to address the times you exhibit racism or defend your whiteness. If your group includes close friends and family, it's harder for them to call you in because they won't want to hurt your feelings. While it's convenient to work with them, it might cause more harm than good. As I stated previously, echo chambers aren't conducive to ally work. Even if you've been working toward allyship for years, you should recognize you're always capable of harming Black women. You need someone who will hold you accountable and guide you toward understanding what you did wrong. That way you can try to lessen the chances of it happening again in the future. If you don't have this level of accountability, your ally journey will stall without you even knowing it. You'll continue exhibiting racism because you haven't changed your behavior and grown as an ally. *How do you feel about sharing your harm with other allies and working through it together? Why is this important in your journey?*

You also must hold other white people accountable for their racism. That means your family, friends, coworkers . . . everybody. It's not simply enough to work on yourself. While these conversations can be painful, they're necessary ally work. If someone around you says something racist, tell them. Let the conversation move from there. Ask other allies how they navigate conversations with people who are an important part of their lives and start doing it. Even if the conversation doesn't go perfectly, keep confronting racist people. You'll get better at it. More importantly, you put them on notice that you don't tolerate racists and will confront them every time it happens. You won't change every mind. However, you'll let them know you're unwilling to stay silent and they can expect a confrontation with you any time they exhibit racist behavior. *What would prevent you from having these conversations? How will you get past those feelings?*

Find a racial justice group that encourages conversations around race but also has policies in place to protect non-white members. That's important. If you're not working with other allies in the group and regularly seeing discussions or readings to help you on your journey, join an additional group. The reason white mentors in "Real Talk" have learned to educate others is because they constantly find new resources to keep them learning and processing their own whiteness. They talk amongst each other about the training—what needs improvement and what works well. Mentors understand that, as allies, they're lifelong learners. Many allies in "Real Talk" have a library of resources they've collected over the years that they pass on to other allies who may be struggling. We regularly post information in "Real Talk," but many other groups and organizations produce great information on topics such as white supremacy, white privilege, systemic racism, and allyship. *How will you keep learning so you continually improve as an ally?* That's why it's important you work with other allies. Compare notes and see what resources they have that you can use and vice versa. Pay attention to the information Black women and women of color in those spaces convey. Oftentimes, they're passing on resources that have only been shared in non-white spaces, so you might not see them otherwise.

Also take note of what they say about white people who have stepped into the racial justice arena. They're not saying anything different than Black women. Yet they command large audiences of white followers. Why are white people following them instead of giving their time and money to Black women speaking and writing about the same topics?

Why are white people more likely to listen to other white people talk about racism than the people actually experiencing it? This is part of your ally work—understanding why white people can easily dismiss Black women when we share our experiences but listen raptly when white people convey stories they've heard from us. There's a definite disconnect there and, for Black women, it comes at both a monetary and a societal cost.

Allies don't just believe Black women. They **follow** Black women. They **support** Black women. That's what we need. Join a racial justice group we lead and commit not only to learning about becoming an ally but listening to us and believing our stories. Don't challenge our experiences and never insert yourself into conversations to defend other white people who have exhibited racism—even if that person is someone close to you. You have to respect them enough to allow them to stumble on their journey and learn from their mistakes. If a white person comes to your defense when you make a mistake, tell them to stop and challenge them about why they tried to prevent you from taking responsibility for your racism. Allow yourself and others to fail and learn from those failures.

Black women don't expect perfect allies. There's no such thing. We don't want allies who strive for perfection. We want allies who know they will harm and understand that the only way to lessen the instances is to keep learning.

REINFORCE YOUR KNOWLEDGE

Use your journal to answer the following questions and discuss how you completed the actions.

Scenario

You're one of the participants in a study about allies. A Black woman nominates you as a friend. They're uncertain how you would respond to racism. They don't know if you're motivated or how you feel about Black women. Score yourself on the following statements from 1 to 9 (1 being the lowest) and explain your scores. What did you learn about yourself?

> *I am interested in hearing about the experiences of Black women.*
>
> *I am comfortable around Black women.*
>
> *I am willing to confront racism to stand up for Black women.*
>
> *I respect Black women.*

Question 1: Think about your emotions and ally work. How will you address the times you feel angry or defensive when you're called a racist or someone supporting white supremacy? How will you work on listening versus defending yourself?

Question 2: How will you address harm with people you know? What are some ways you can start the conversation when you hear another white person being racist?

Action

Join a racial justice group led by a Black woman. You can join more than one. This can be either an in-person or online group you find on Facebook or another online space. In addition, find another group that is addressing specific issues mentioned in this chapter.

Chapter 3
OBSTACLES MEAN LESSONS

Finding growth in your discomfort

Discomfort and education go hand in hand. As you begin to understand how you contribute to racism and the oppression of Black women, you'll feel uncomfortable learning about your own complicity. However, if you increase your knowledge and internalize the information, you'll become an effective ally. A 2019 research study, which discusses the effect of knowledge on recognizing racism, proves my point. In this study, social liberals and social conservatives both were given a scenario in which a policeman shot a man. In some cases, participants were told the man was Black. In others, he was white. Researchers assumed the social liberals would believe more than the social conservatives that racism drove the policeman's decision to shoot. Given that assumption, they wanted to know what effect, if any, learning about white privilege would have on social conservatives. Participants in both groups were randomly assigned either reading a statement about white privilege or a controlled reading about the benefits of routine. *How does understanding white privilege help you as an ally? What challenges do/did you have with recognizing your own white privilege?*

Everyone was then given a detailed police report of the event, which I'll summarize for you here. The policeman was responding to reports of a robbery and given a general description of the suspect. He was also told the man may be armed. The officer sees a man fitting the description several blocks from the scene of the robbery, carrying a grocery bag. The man runs into a backyard when he sees the officer exit his patrol car. The policeman confronts him in the yard and pulls his gun. He tells the man to drop the bag and put his hands up. The man reaches his hand inside the grocery bag, and the officer shoots him. There are no witnesses to the shooting. The suspect didn't have a gun but did have a knife strapped to his ankle. When shown his picture, the robbery victim couldn't positively identify the man as the one who robbed him. When asked why he fired, the officer responded that he felt like he was "in a cage with the Hulk" and he would have gotten hurt if he hadn't shot him. The man is hospitalized in the ICU. *Let's assume the suspect is Black. What assumptions does the officer make in this scenario? The scenario doesn't say whether the man who was shot actually was the robber. How would you feel if he were the robber? What if he weren't?*

The results of the first study showed that, regardless of political ideology, when the suspect was a Black man, participants' level of perception of racism during the encounter increased if they learned about white privilege. They blamed the suspect less and the officer more. If the suspect were white, the levels didn't change.

The second part of the study asked participants to consider if they were on a jury hearing this case. This time, participants were told the suspect was a Black man. After reading about white privilege, participants again showed an increased perception of racism and a decreased blame of the suspect.[8]

This study shows us that education can change the minds of white people. That's why it's so important that you seek out resources to educate yourself. It's how you engage with racism both within yourself and in others. Simply arguing without possessing the groundwork of relevant information will make you an ineffective ally. You may only have one chance to discuss racism with the person you're trying to educate. Make sure you have resources to give them. You won't change every mind, but go into each conversation attempting to make them think about their racist behaviors. Giving them concrete evidence about racism is one way to do that. The more you learn, the better you'll become at recognizing which resources to utilize in a particular situation. Remember to work with other white people or even check in with an accountability partner after your encounter. Debrief so you know what you did right and what you can improve

8   Cooley, E., Brown-Iannuzzi, J., & Cottrell, D. J. (2019). Liberals perceive more racism than conservatives when police shoot Black men-But, reading about White privilege increases perceived racism, and shifts attributions of guilt, regardless of political ideology. *Journal of Experimental Social Psychology*, 85. https://doi.org/10.1016/j.jesp.2019.103885

upon. This isn't the time for ego. Don't let constructive criticism prevent you from continuing to do ally work.

Learning about white privilege triggers white people. *Why are white people defensive and uncomfortable about their white privilege? What does acknowledging it mean for them?* That's why it's important to fight the discomfort of realizing how much your white skin makes your life easier. That's not to say you don't have hardships, but your white privilege gives you more avenues to overcome them than Black people. *What are some of the ways white privilege makes your life easier?* Prior to the aforementioned study, participants who didn't understand or think about white privilege probably pushed back against the idea that their skin color benefited them in any way. *What are some reasons white people don't believe they have white privilege?* Everyone faces hardships throughout their lives. However, white people don't endure these challenges because of their skin color. Roadblocks aren't thrown in their path, preventing them from achieving their goals simply because they're white. This is the difference between what I constantly face and what you as a white person face. Unlike you, my difficulties are compounded because I'm Black.

Another study researched why white people responded to hearing about their racial (white) privilege by claiming more personal hardships. They believed that conveying their own struggles in life would lessen the amount of white privilege they actually possessed. Researchers divided participants into two groups. In the first experiment, one group was exposed to evidence about white privilege, and the other group wasn't. Participants exposed to information about white privilege claimed more hardships to prove that, while white privilege did exist, they didn't personally benefit from it. Researchers believed that participants saw white privilege as a threat to their sense of self. ***How would acknowledging white privilege threaten your sense of self?*** The study also found that claims of increased hardship also decreased the support white people gave to policies that would help fight racial inequities. Therefore, it's not surprising that belief in white privilege on a personal level also meant more affirmative action support.

In the second experiment, researchers found that white participants who were asked to rank categories related to personal values important to them—called self-affirmation—didn't claim additional hardships when given evidence about white privilege. In fact, they claimed less hardship. Researchers believed self-affirmation gave participants a strong sense of self. Therefore, they didn't need to claim hardships to distance themselves from white privilege. The study showed the importance of both white people understanding white privilege but also the need to prevent them from feeling threatened by the knowledge.[9] ***How would self-affirmation help you as an ally? What values do you have that will help you grow as an ally?*** Recognizing white privilege is a necessary part of this work.

---

9   Phillips, L. T. & Lowery, B. S. (2015). The hard-knock life? Whites claim hardships in response to racial inequity. *Journal of Experimental Social Psychology, (61),* 12–18. http://dx.doi.org/10.1016/j.jesp.2015.06.008

White people who don't understand what it means to be an ally to Black women probably believe that a passive education will get them to the finish line. Many are afraid of saying anything for fear of hearing criticism. *How does white privilege play into the idea that passive education is allyship?* Racial justice work isn't much different than any other type of education. However, you must understand that discomfort is a key to successful allyship. Sometimes that discomfort means you've delved into new territory; so you're nervous about engaging with another white person using the information you've just learned but haven't yet internalized. This is the first time you've had this particular conversation, and you're not as confident about the subject as you'll be if you keep practicing. Other times, the discomfort stems from making a mistake. You're terrified you'll be called in for that error in judgment.

Somehow you've worked yourself up to the point where you view any discomfort negatively, and that's not the case at all. *Name a time in your life when you were uncomfortable but the outcome made the discomfort worth it.* Allies use their discomfort—whether it be anger, fear or apprehension—to understand how they're feeling in that moment and whether they're centering their feelings to the detriment of fighting racism. You can't avoid discomfort. In doing so, you're ignoring the feelings you must acknowledge so that you know when you're on track as an ally. Those feelings are simply growing pains. Don't allow them to stagnate your progress. Once you've gotten into the rhythm of working on your allyship, you'll recognize the harm caused by inaction.

You also will be able to point it out in other white people. Remember your goal as an ally is to be anti-racist. It's never enough to say, "I'm not racist." You must actively work to fight for us. Otherwise, your passivity and silence will allow racism to continue to flourish. In that environment, Black women can't progress, and we will never achieve equality.

White people are accustomed to their comfort being prioritized over Black lives. When they're asked to move outside of that bubble and address racism in themselves or other people, they shrink away from it. If they're afraid to speak up in a private online group where only members see their interactions, how does that translate into real-life situations? I think it's safe to say they're not speaking up at all. Their idea of allyship is skewed. They're too busy avoiding the real work of getting uncomfortable to actually learn how to be effective allies.

When I remove white women from "Real Talk" because they refuse to engage, oftentimes they send Facebook messages asking me why they are no longer members. One woman who begged for reentry said, "But I learn so much from the reading." She's convinced herself that perusing posts about racism means she's actually doing the work. In fact, her support in the fight against racism is at zero. If you're caught in the theory of racism and ignore the reality, you've decided that your comfort is more important than fighting for Black women. *Where do you see yourself struggling with discomfort during this process? How will you work through it?* There are two sides to learning about racism—the theoretical side and the experiential side. I've always focused on the experiential—or action-based—aspect of allyship. That's where the real work resides. There's no in-between. Either you're an ally who understands what we're up against and is motivated to take a stand or you're simply another white person sitting on the sidelines protecting your whiteness. *How will you stay committed to the discomfort of ally work?*

I regularly remind white people that Black people are uncomfortable all the time. I've endured toxic whiteness my entire life. I've encountered racism for as long as I can remember. It's exhausting to live in a society where white people constantly judge you based on your skin color and do so without any threat of repercussions. *Imagine if your existence were constantly disrupted by people who could abuse and marginalize you at their will. How would you feel?* That's how Black women exist. That's why it's so important that potential allies get off the sidelines and speak up. Racists have had free rein for too long. We have to take that power away from them. That means you must be willing to battle your discomfort so that these racist systems start to crumble and racism is finally defeated.

If you pay attention to real potential allies in those spaces who share their own experiences about anti-racist work, you'll realize that simply showing up doesn't count. You should notice that, while they're in motion learning and stretching their boundaries, you're sitting around reading articles. *What fears do you have about participating in discussions that include sharing your own experiences?* While I understand the hesitation to speak up, this is when you must embrace that discomfort. You don't grow as an ally unless you make a conscious decision to challenge yourself. That means you push yourself in ways that force you out of your comfort zone.

Becoming an ally isn't easy, and continually growing can be challenging. White people new to this work tend to get stuck in the reading phase. Other allies are giving you resources to begin your education about racism. That's the easy part. Reading about racism is necessary but ultimately passive work. While it's an essential step in allyship, you won't change yourself or others simply by collecting articles or watching documentaries. I've had white people argue this point with me. *How do you know you're changing if you haven't actually engaged with other white people and pushed yourself to the point of discomfort? What actions would you take to prevent yourself from getting stuck?* I doubt that many white people reading about racism see themselves in those words. An accountability partner or affinity group will keep you on task and help you find that balance between discomfort and growth. That's the reason you can't do this work alone. You won't hold yourself to the standards needed to fight against racism. White people who have convinced themselves otherwise have no real interest in learning and growing through this process. They will never be real allies we can count on to fight for us.

That's why I need you to commit yourself to read *and* take action using the information you've learned. The only effective way to do this work is by regularly reaching out to other white people who are also learning to become allies.

It's impossible to fully understand your complicity in racism without someone calling you in when you exhibit that behavior. Racism and white privilege are commonplace in white culture—so common that you either don't see the harm it causes us, or you're used to making excuses about the violence and oppression we suffer. **_Does that statement make you uncomfortable? Why?_** When you begin discussing racism and your part in that institution, you'll feel uncomfortable. You'll get defensive. **_What can you do to push through these feelings?_**

You should expect discomfort doing this work. However, the longer you consciously move through becoming anti-racist, the better you'll become at handling those feelings. That discomfort helps you stretch in ways you otherwise wouldn't. That's the lesson you must learn and share with other allies. Discomfort means you're entering a phase of allyship that requires you to do more work. So you might need to check in with other white people or sit back and listen while a Black woman shares her experiences. Or both. If you know you're lacking in an area of your education, find the needed resources to fill that gap and add that knowledge to the arsenal you use to educate other white people and confront racism. **_How will you seek out new information? What steps would you take so you're continually educating yourself?_**

It's okay to be afraid. I would be surprised if you weren't apprehensive about the conversations you'll have in the future. The idea of exposing yourself and confronting others is daunting. Even your internal dialogues where you admit your own racism can be terrifying. This is where you push through the discomfort and admit that you actively participate in white supremacy and racism. You need to acknowledge that you'll always be potentially harmful to Black women. Countless times, I've witnessed seasoned allies misstep because their attraction to whiteness won over their commitment to racial justice work. When that happens, these allies don't quit. They admit their harm and work through that challenge to lessen the chances of it happening again. That is how you become a better ally. Every lesson you learn is one you can add to your library of resources to educate another white person struggling with that same concept. Remember that allyship is about teaching yourself as well as others.

Is it scary to have those conversations? Of course. Fight through that fear. Keep going. *What scares you about the conversations you'll have with other white people?* The worst thing you can do is allow that fear and discomfort to win. As you become a more experienced ally, you'll understand those feelings are necessary to help you grow in this work. You want to move outside of your white-centric bubble every chance you get. You can't do that by just taking in information. You have to both process it and act upon it. In this case, you're learning about yourself and also reaching out to white people with whom you can share your knowledge. *What are some ideas you already have about addressing your own racism?*

We've all encountered situations in our lives that made us uncomfortable. Every one of us has goals and achievements we want to reach. Reaching—and surpassing—them requires us to embrace the discomfort that comes along with moving outside of the box that prevents us from reaching the next level. *What are the ramifications for Black women if you allow your discomfort to prevent you from learning about racism and speaking up?* Think about a situation that made you uncomfortable, but you pushed through anyway. What was on the other side? That other side contains the growth that comes from overcoming any difficult situation. We don't move forward unless we experience discomfort. We do this in our daily lives. We do this when we're promoted or change careers. We do this when we experience new cultures. It can be something as simple as exercising and increasing the level of difficulty every time. Although exerting yourself through exercise is a physical discomfort, it's still entering a new level. Either way, you're now in a place where you're no longer comfortable. You'll either push through or quit. Commit to pushing yourself until you emerge on the other side. *Why is it important to reach the other side of your discomfort? What should you do once you get there?*

Several years ago I went to therapy because I was struggling with feelings of anger regarding a situation at work. One of my managers, a white man, was a misogynist racist. I did the right thing and told my other manager, and he in turn did nothing. For the next eight years, I endured the ramifications of speaking up for myself. I was blackballed the rest of my time there. I wasn't respected for my work, and I couldn't get promoted. I was labeled a difficult employee who was bad at her job. I saw a therapist to process all the anger I felt about the unfairness of my situation. It was extremely uncomfortable to tell my stories of humiliation and disappointment, but I knew if I didn't get them out, I would never get past the situation. I'm much better for seeking help.

Replace my therapist with an accountability partner or affinity group in your case. If you're feeling such a level of discomfort that you get stuck, work through that with another white person. You would be surprised at how many other people have experienced those same feelings. They can provide you with tools to process that situation and move through it. *What lessons could you learn about yourself when you work through discomfort with another white person?*

Take note each time you feel uncomfortable as an ally. Talk through the situation and pinpoint when you felt discomfort and why. *Were you uncomfortable when another person called you in for your racist behavior? Were you uncomfortable when you called someone else in?* Ally work requires engaging in situations even when those situations will cause you stress. However, you've spent your entire life not acknowledging racism and your part in that system. You've centered your comfort over the equality of Black women your entire lives. That realization should make you uncomfortable. Guilt may also come with discomfort. You'll feel guilty about racism you've exhibited or witnessed. Process those feelings, too. Whatever emotions arise, make sure you're not centering yourself if you must take action.

How will you ensure you're not centering yourself when you feel uncomfortable?

For example, your accountability partner takes you aside to talk about your comment, "Dr. King never would have supported Black Lives Matter." (By the way, this is a common statement white people make when talking about this organization.) She asks how you know what Dr. King would support. She challenges your knowledge about Black Lives Matter and questions why you would disregard such an important movement that protests violence against Black people in this country. You might feel defensive and uncomfortable. *How would you respond? What can you do so you don't make this mistake in the future?* You may feel attacked at this moment because you didn't intend to dismiss the Black Lives Matter movement. However, remember that the impact of your words is more important than your intentions. Look at your discomfort in this situation as an indication that you've taken a wrong turn in your allyship. Your feelings should come as a warning that you've stepped off the path toward true allyship and taken another path that led you to make an uninformed, racist comment. Use your discomfort to think about that call-in. *What else can you do in this scenario to educate yourself about this movement?*

Allyship means action. So remember that, while you're educating yourself, you're also preparing to teach others. Calling other white people in will cause you significant discomfort. However, call-ins also help you learn about yourself. *What can you learn about yourself when you call other white people in?* Every time you work with another white person, you should discover more about your own challenges. These revelations help you constantly improve as an ally. Your knowledge from these experiences, as well as from constantly learning about different subjects related to anti-racism, will be important tools when you're confronting other white people on their racism. That's why you must take advantage of all the ways you can learn.

Keep in mind that no matter how much you learn, you'll experience times when your attempt at educating another white person fails because you didn't yet know enough about the topic to have an in-depth discussion. That's okay. You don't need all the answers when you're trying to teach others. You can say, "Let me find some resources on this topic, and I'll get back to you." *How can you be better prepared next time?* That gives you time to regroup and touch base with other allies who may have knowledge on the topic to share with you. You also obtain more information to add to your library of resources as you move forward. Regardless of how prepared you feel, be ready for the inevitable discomfort you'll feel when dealing with white people who react angrily to your words. *How can you respond to a white person who gets angry when you confront them about their racism? What if that person is a family member or close friend?* Be ready to move through uncomfortable situations as an ally. Discomfort shouldn't prevent you from doing this work. Black people exist in a white-centric society that doesn't make space for us to live freely. That's the very definition of discomfort. It won't kill you to experience these feelings if it means you're learning how to fight with us.

That's not to say you should jump into the deep end of allyship. It's a process, and feeling uncomfortable is just one step in your journey. Set goals for yourself. Consider what you've learned and what you struggle to understand. If you're feeling unsettled, work through that with another ally. Your job is to figure out which part of what you heard makes you uneasy. Be honest with yourself about why you feel that way. If it touches a nerve because you see your own racist beliefs or oppressive behaviors, push through it. ***Why is it important that you recognize your own racism?*** White people begin allyship thinking they haven't harmed Black women—at least not in any significant way. They believe, because their actions were unintentional, they're also forgivable.

That's why white people often say they didn't intend to hurt us. However, your intentions don't prevent the violence of your racism. You'll anger us, and that will make you uncomfortable. ***How will you handle your discomfort when a Black woman shows anger toward you?*** I've encountered countless allies who've lectured me about my tone when speaking to them. If Black women were nicer, more white people would be allies, right? No, they wouldn't. Left unchecked and unchallenged, white people will go about their white-centered lives without a thought about how their whiteness affects Black women. It takes a conscious decision not to put themselves first. It takes fighting their discomfort to strive to see us as equals and want to fight alongside us.

Use your discomfort as a gauge of your progress. If you're never uncomfortable, you're not pushing to educate yourself and others. ***What are some ways you can use your***

discomfort to your advantage? When you're moving outside of the comfort of whiteness, you'll be surprised at how often you've previously retreated into that box over the smallest conflicts. You can decide either to retreat into your bubble or listen—which is a cornerstone of allyship—and learn from us. Otherwise, what good are you? You're saying your inaction is allyship, but we would never define it that way. Allies are constantly in motion. They listen to new concepts, process their discomfort, and fight to overcome it. They discuss those feelings with other white people and teach the ones who haven't yet been exposed to this new information. The key is, if that information makes them uncomfortable, real allies don't dismiss it. ***What can you do so you don't dismiss or disbelieve information that makes you uncomfortable?*** Allies keep digging until they emerge with new knowledge they can use to educate other white people.

REINFORCE YOUR KNOWLEDGE

Use your journal to answer the following questions and discuss how you completed the actions.

Scenario

You're one of the participants in the aforementioned study. Decide if you are a social liberal or a social conservative. Reread the shooting incident and answer the following questions looking through a racial justice lens: Why do you think the policeman tried to stop the suspect? Why do you think the policeman fired his weapon? Why did the suspect run? If you were on a jury and the policeman were on trial, what questions would you have for your fellow jurors during deliberations?

Question 1: How will you prevent yourself from quitting because you're uncomfortable after getting called in for exhibiting racism?

Question 2: What happens if you become complacent and avoid discomfort in racial justice work?

Action

Discuss with your accountability partner or affinity group ways that you can embrace discomfort. How will you keep growing? What can you do to help each other work through times where you're outside of your comfort zone and struggling to move forward?

Part II

THE COST OF WHITENESS

····································

Week 2

Chapter 4

GET OUT OF YOUR HEAD

Listening without defensiveness and white tears

As an ally, one of the most important lessons you should work through is actively listening without defensiveness and what we call "white tears." White tears aren't literal tears—at least not usually. They're emotions white people show when you realize just how difficult racism is—for white people. Defensiveness is a weapon white people wield when you're confronted with your racism. You use it in an attempt to ignore how you've harmed us. Defensiveness and white tears have no place in ally work. They prevent you from any learning or accountability. **Have you ever exhibited white tears? When? How?**

Years ago, a white woman in "Real Talk" was one of the most vocal white people I've ever encountered when it came to calling in others. If you watched from a distance, you would believe she was a strong ally for Black women. She had the script down. She regurgitated all the right words in every situation. On closer inspection, she fell short of being a true ally to us. Why? Because she didn't like being called in when she made mistakes. As a matter of fact, she *refused* to be called in, stating only Black women could teach her anything. She claimed to have nothing to learn from other white people. *What's the problem with asking only Black women to educate her?* This isn't allyship. It doesn't matter how loudly you stand up for us or how effectively you confront racists. If you won't address your own racism, you're dangerous to Black people and the anti-racism movement. If you refuse to acknowledge your harm, you'll keep repeating it. *How would you prevent yourself from refusing to admit harm?* We don't want those kinds of white people as potential allies. If you refuse to acknowledge your racism when asked to do so, we have no place for you in this work.

So what happened to this white woman? She dropped out of sight after she was confronted yet again about her racism and performative allyship (I'll discuss "performative allyship" in Chapter 10). Instead of working to better herself, she chose to retreat—but not before burdening a Black woman with educating her, then refusing to listen to anything this woman had to say. *What could this white woman have done differently after she was called in?*

White allies should strive to continuously listen and learn. However, they won't agree with everything they hear. It's not because the information is wrong. It's because white people's defenses go up when they hear information that they believe unfairly criticizes them and other white people. One common example I've encountered is the "Not all white people" responses. If I say, "White people voted for Donald Trump because they support his white supremacist ideology," inevitably a white person will respond with, "Not all white people voted for Donald Trump." This comment is usually followed by some sort of nonsense about alienating potential allies. The problem with getting defensive and saying "Not all white people" is that, instead of listening to the actual context, you've decided it's much more important to deflect from the conversation and make it about you. If you didn't vote for Trump, then I'm not talking about you. It's that simple.

However, if I say white people benefit from white privilege and you come at me with the same "Not all white people" response, we'll have a different conversation. That's because all white people benefit from white privilege (I'll explain white privilege in the next chapter). ***How does that statement make you feel? Give an example of how you personally benefit from white privilege.*** White privilege has been thoroughly researched and proven. Yet the idea that white people haven't gotten to where they are strictly through hard work galls them. When I'm discussing white privilege with white people, I like to recommend Peggy McIntosh's essay "White Privilege: Unpacking the Invisible Knapsack." She provides us with a succinct explanation. Google the title and read the entire essay. ***Have you ever thought or said, "Not all white people"? What was the context? Why did you say it? What could you have done instead?***

Here are some short examples of white privilege to get you started:

- *You have a positive relationship with police and don't worry about being profiled or harassed.*

- *You learned from history books focused on white American and white European history.*

- *Employers don't discriminate against your skin color, hairstyle, or name.*

- *Your home may be valued higher by a real estate appraiser because you're white.*

- *You see your race positively represented in the media.*

- *You regularly see people who look like you in positions of power.*

How does this list make you feel? Do you disagree with any of them?

That's why white privilege is easy for you to overlook. Unless you're actively seeking information about unfair housing practices or the whitewashing of Black history, you go along never thinking about what you gain by white privilege and what Black people lose because of it.

The media also plays a hand in the continued oppression of Black people. Think about the numerous times white people have called the police on one of us—the many videos of white people threatening us and the hashtags that followed. Remember #BBQBecky? She's the San Francisco woman who called the police on two Black men barbequing in the park. What's especially offensive about these 911 calls is that white people know that they're usually believed by law enforcement. It doesn't matter that the Black person has done nothing wrong. They're also aware that phone call could result in police violence against us.

A 2020 study examined the lack of connection between these 911 calls to any actions to address larger issues of social conditions such as racism. Researchers looked at these phone calls and the social media posts and news coverage that followed. They examined the narratives about these incidents and focused on how the story was told and descriptions of the people involved. Researchers wanted to know if the use of hashtags connected stories to social issues. What they found was news coverage used hashtags to sensationalize a story, but they rarely delved into the racist behavior of the white person who perpetrated the act. They didn't investigate the reasons the hashtags were created, nor did they report on the relationship between these calls and the racism behind them.

Researchers found that news organizations jumped on the use of hashtags and monikers. They focused on the actions of the 911 callers but failed to look at the more important meaning of why the social media posts were created—as a means of "Black resistance and commentary." For example, the *San Francisco Examiner* reported on a white woman calling 911 because a Black girl didn't have a permit to sell water outside her home. The Black mother recorded the incident and dubbed the woman #PermitPatty. The newspaper took up the hashtag and reported on the incident. However, they didn't ask the mother or her daughter how the encounter made them feel. Instead, they tied #PermitPatty to #BBQBecky because the situations occurred relatively close to each other. They didn't consider discussing how racism played a part in this incident. Instead they downplayed #BBQBecky by saying only that she deserved the name. The *San Francisco Chronicle* referred to "Becky" as a derogatory name for a white woman, but they didn't go any further than that vague explanation. News agencies instead report about videos going viral and the number of views. They leave out the human consequences behind those racist encounters.

The study goes on to explain how these hashtags and monikers are more than ways to call out racist white people. Black people want to disrupt the system by bringing the incidents to light. We know that these encounters could easily turn violent—even deadly—for us. When the media focuses on the popularity of the hashtags, they diminish the importance of understanding the racism behind the acts. Instead of saying the white person was racist, reporters gave other excuses as to why they behaved in such a way that may have just *looked* racist.

Researchers found that, because police action often was missing in the videos, the media didn't take the situations as seriously. Reporters didn't discuss the possibility of physical violence and the ramifications for the Black people in these videos. In fact, a Black man who was prevented from entering his own apartment building by a white woman because she didn't believe he lived here said the police treated him like a criminal until they saw his video. That video also went viral.

In a *USA Today* article, researchers found one of the few instances where reporters asked the victim how she was affected by the incident. A white male pool manager called 911 because he didn't believe the woman belonged in that neighborhood and had no right to swim in the pool. The article did report that she and her family were traumatized by the incident but went no further than that.

What we remember from these stories is whether the perpetrator is fired or experienced any consequences at all for their actions. However, in many cases, the news media doesn't even use their real names. They stick with the hashtag or moniker when reporting about them. It downplays the seriousness of calling 911—a call you should make only in real emergencies. Researchers found that news agencies didn't report on social issues connected with these occurrences and provided no context so that their readers would understand the racial issues Black people on social media try to expose through these hashtags.[10]

This study highlights a pattern of the media's refusal to call out racists. In fact, the media has been instrumental in portraying Black people as violent, aggressive animals. This isn't a coincidence but a result of newsrooms comprised of mostly white people bringing their own implicit biases into the stories they cover. It's no wonder that the majority of white Americans see Black women as lazy welfare queens and Black men as hypersexual predators. The media gives an inaccurate, one-sided portrayal of us, and there are no indications that commentary

10   Gutsche, R. E., Cong, X., Pan, F., Sun, Y. & DeLoach, L. (2020). #DiminishingDiscrimination: The symbolic annihilation of race and racism in news hashtags of 'calling 911 on Black people.' *Journalism.* https://doi.org/10.1177/1464884920919279

will ever change. If you only consider the point of reference from the media when seeing Black people protesting the latest murder of a Black person at the hands of the police, you might believe that every Black person participated in rioting and not one was hoping for a peaceful demonstration. I'll go one even further. The media chose to conduct such a one-sided portrayal of those protests because sporadic violence is much more compelling coverage than giving that time to balanced reporting and explaining why people were marching in the first place.

We see this play out repeatedly in the press. They ignore the reasons behind the anger that drives Black people to the streets and focus on any behavior that shows us as subhuman and not worthy of equality. The media lacks checks and balances when it comes to reporting on racism in this country. All-white newsrooms will never provide an accurate depiction of reporting the backstories and histories of Black people, instead highlighting any negativity they find about us. They lend credence to the racist ideology of many white people. We expect the media to provide views from both sides. However, Black people are rarely given the benefit of the doubt. More often than not, we're seen as the perpetrator and deserving of any outcome—even death. White people excuse white supremacy and racism, even in the newsroom. Reporters and the editors who are supposed to question their reporting aren't held to any standard related to conveying information about Black issues because there aren't any Black people in those spaces to challenge their reporting.

The media is but one example of how racism and white supremacy drive harmful narratives about Black people.

Even if Black people confronted these white reporters, most of the journalists would defend their reporting and dismiss any questioning of what they put into print or broadcasted on television. In my experience, white people vehemently defend themselves when they're criticized about their defense of whiteness. They're so wrapped up in convincing us they haven't received any advantages because they're white, that they won't even listen when we present them with compelling evidence to the contrary. This "white defensiveness" is just another way for them to turn a blind eye to the unfavorable advantages they have simply for being white. They will defend anything. How many of us have heard white people say a Black person should have complied when confronted by law enforcement, when we've seen video after video of us doing just that and still being beaten or murdered? But they don't want to hear it. How many times have we heard white people say, "We don't know what happened before the video" after watching a Black person gunned down by police? White people will defend law enforcement because they aren't on the receiving end of that racial violence.

Reparations is another topic that triggers white defensiveness. When I say that Black people still live under a cloud of systemic oppression as a direct result of slavery, white people don't believe me. Instead, they claim white people also face discrimination, so we shouldn't need any unfair advantages to succeed in this country. They refuse to acknowledge that their whiteness allows them to start ahead of us and finish before us. Black people have demanded reparations for generations. Yet it falls on deaf ears. Ronald Reagan signed the Civil Liberties

Act of 1988 and granted $20,000 in reparations to survivors of Japanese internment camps that were in existence from 1942 to 1945. Black people were enslaved in this country for almost 250 years, creating a system of oppression that continues to this day. Yet we deserve no monies for the damage the legacy of slavery still does to our community. White people defend their nonsupport of reparations by saying we weren't slaves, blatantly ignoring the history of oppression that existed through laws, racial violence, and intimidation to keep Black people as second-class citizens. White people will defend the politics and laws still in place that create two very different realities—a Black one and a white one—and claim that there's no difference between them. Most Black schools operate with far less funding than white ones. Yet white people defend the gap between graduation rates as a failing of those students instead of a system working exactly the way it was intended. White people will defend statistics that tell us Black women die at a higher rate from breast cancer by saying those women just needed to take better care of themselves or visit a doctor earlier to increase their survival rates. They will readily defend medical racism as nonexistent because they've never witnessed it. This is the gist of much of the white defensiveness I've witnessed. White people will claim Black people exaggerate our experiences of racism because *they* haven't seen those incidents firsthand. However, it's impossible to recognize a behavior that they regularly uphold and protect. For many white people, racism is as natural as breathing.

White people must understand the motives behind your willingness to defend racism. As an ally, your job is to call out these white people and educate them. I won't sugarcoat call-ins.

They're not fun. They're probably embarrassing, and no one likes being on the receiving end of them. However, learning from your mistakes keeps you on track. Without them, you would blindly go along, believing you're doing everything right. No one actually doing the work to become an ally will completely avoid harming Black women. We just want you to actively *try* not to harm us. That's the best you'll be able to do. **How do you feel about being called in for your racist behavior? How will you actively listen instead of defending your actions?**

Don't fall into the trap that you don't need to learn from your mistakes. It's tempting to quickly apologize and say, "I understand what I did. Let's just move on." Allyship doesn't work that way. You learn by meticulously moving through the process of understanding why you exhibited racist behavior and how to make amends for the pain you caused. That's why I keep repeating how important it is to have an affinity group or accountability partner who can help you understand where you went wrong. That's how you progress as an ally. Don't be afraid to make mistakes. You can expect to make numerous missteps on your journey to becoming an ally.

One of your first inclinations when you're called in might be to say you're sorry. What are you sorry for at this point? Do you even know? You just know a Black woman is angry because of something you said. Where is the work in that? Where is the processing so you don't repeat that mistake? I'm offended when white women apologize to me for their harm but refuse to have any further discussion. So what they're saying to me is, "I've apologized to you. That's all I'm doing. Take it or leave it." I'll leave it, thanks. That apology is insincere and superficial.

***How do you feel when someone apologizes to you but doesn't
really address the pain they caused? How would you respond
to them?*** It's a knee-jerk reaction to the embarrassment you
feel because a Black woman called you out about your racism. Oftentimes, you just want the entire situation to go away.
There's nothing in that mindset that says "ally." It exhibits white
fragility, and that's counterproductive to your growth. You
don't decide the way in which you make amends. You work
with another white person so you can understand what you
did wrong and how it affected the Black woman on the receiving end of that harm. This process helps you understand the
violent effects of your words. That's what you need to know. A
simple apology will never be enough. ***How will you commit to
actively listening and not defending yourself? What can you
say to yourself to keep on track when you're called in?***

When white people are called in for racism, you oftentimes
try to downplay or dismiss the seriousness of your words or
actions. That tactic might have worked for you in the past,
but this behavior won't cut it if you want to become an ally. If
you're making light of your mistake, you're not serious about
fighting for us. I must be able to trust you to do the work
when you know you need to make amends. It shouldn't be a
battle. You shouldn't argue with me when I tell you how your
actions have affected me. ***What harm do you cause when
you defend your actions?*** This is the time to internalize my
words and process them. Don't say that's not what you meant
or it wasn't your intention to hurt me. Always keep in mind
that your impact is always greater than your intentions. That

means your intended result doesn't matter nearly as much as how your words and actions affected me.

Get in the habit of gauging the potential impact of your words or actions beforehand. It's too late to explain your intentions once you've already exhibited racism. If you think more carefully about your words and actions, you'll hurt Black women less. *What tools can you use to think through possible harm before you exhibit it?* The goal is to be able to recognize your potential missteps beforehand and help other white people learn this important lesson, too. Be prepared for them to exhibit the same defensiveness you've seen in yourself. Like you, they will double down. Again, it's a process. You have to learn how to recognize the emotions that are detrimental to allyship.

Once you're called in, sit and listen to where you went wrong. Don't interrupt. Don't shut down because you're angry. Don't get defensive. That defensiveness prevents you from listening. It's tempting to try to explain yourself, but refrain from doing this. Instead, admit that you have work to do. And that's okay. That work is a much-needed part of your progress. I know it's tempting to get defensive and angry, but both of those emotions will prevent you from learning from your mistakes. Fight those feelings so they don't control what you hear and the lesson you should be learning. That way, you're becoming a better ally by acquiring the tools to teach other white people. *What are some of the tools you learn from listening when you're called in?* It's one thing for you to fight for Black women. We also need you to educate other white people on their own journeys. *How will*

you start teaching other white people? What are some stories or lessons you've already learned that you can share?

Allies also understand they should never defend themselves or other white people when addressing racism. When you're called in, don't make that experience about your own feelings. In other words, don't center yourself. It's about the Black woman you harmed. Respond with "I understand," or even say "Thank you." Admit you have work to do. Any response you make to your call-in should be an affirmation of your harm and a commitment to work through it. That way, you come out on the other side with newfound knowledge and a renewed sense of commitment to your journey. **Why is it important you understand you have work to do?** Say you'll do the work to gain the knowledge and do better the next time. Take some time to think about your error. Ask other allies to process with you so you can understand where you failed. This is the time when you're working through the harm you caused. This process can take several days. Remember to take notes or, if you're processing electronically, save the conversation. **Why is this important?** Don't rush to finish this part. The point of processing what happened is to learn more about yourself and make amends to the person affected by your actions.

Make sure you have another white person help you craft an apology. Allies fall into the trap of making the apology too much about them and not enough about us. You want the apology centered on the Black woman and the harm you caused her. Even if it's a situation where you won't be able to deliver the apology, it's important that you craft one anyway. Processing and writing down what you learned helps you solidify those lessons, which is an important part of allyship. *Why is making amends an important part of allyship?* As you progress through your ally journey, you'll know when you caused harm even if you weren't called in for it. When this happens, call yourself in and ask another white person to work with you. It's important that person can be honest with you. They can tell you without any hesitation that you screwed up. They can point out when and where it happened. They can bluntly explain to you where you went wrong. That's what you need to keep learning and growing as an ally.

I've witnessed many new allies struggle over every bit of information and internalize every lesson. They didn't want to say they made a mistake. They wouldn't admit their own racism. I was actually surprised when they kept going. Yet they did. Years later, these white people are some of the most effective allies and ones I regularly count on to educate others. They shed copious white tears, but they refused to quit. These allies held on to every emotion they had when they were called in for their racism. They cried. They got angry. They became defensive. They shut down. They lashed out. These are the white people you wouldn't think would succeed. Yet today they're still doing the work. They readily share stories about their own ally failures so newer allies know that even people doing this work for years still make mistakes. *How will you keep on track when you get angry and want to quit?*

Allies who fought to keep going even when they felt like they did everything wrong oftentimes are the first allies to come to the defense of Black women. They've made every mistake and continue to misstep, although much less often.

They've learned about their own racism and decided they will fight that part of themselves so that they can do the work of dismantling it in others. They readily tell their ally horror stories to other white people. They step up and teach other allies how to recognize these violent beliefs in themselves. These allies stay vigilant when it comes to doing the work because it's too easy to become arrogant or lazy.

When white women in "Real Talk" are called into the "Mending Room," they're assisted with processing their harm. This space isn't punitive. It's educational. That's what a call-in should be—a way for an ally to understand where they went wrong so they can do better next time. **Why is it important that you're learning when you're called in?** Think of processing and making amends as taking continuing-education classes. They're classes you'll revisit again and again. A call-in isn't done to berate or belittle you. It's to explain where you went wrong so you can become a better ally to us. That's it.

Will you encounter Black women who are angry at you? Of course. We have every right to be angry with you when you expose us to your racism. However, that's no excuse for you to quit. Your job is always to listen to the harm you've caused, work through it with your accountability partner, and learn from that experience. You should never tone police the messenger, especially if that messenger is a Black woman. **How do you harm Black women when you tone police?** As Black women, we're always criticized with the "You're so angry" trope. It's how white people dismiss our valid emotions about being treated as less than white people. So of course we're angry. Think about that when you exhibit racism and a Black woman calls you in. We don't have to explain ourselves nicely. We might yell at you. Our anger is justified and includes an education for you. Both the feelings we express to you and the pain you hear in our words are important lessons.

Allies have to take advantage of call-ins to help create an inventory of your racism. *If you had to take an inventory of your own racism, what would it look like? How have you exhibited racism?* When you take note of your racism, it gives you a chance to be honest with yourself about your racist beliefs. That's the only way you can address your racism and have any chance of becoming an effective ally. That means if you're called in because you're being racist, don't deny it. *Why is it important to admit your racism?* If you refuse to admit you've exhibited racism, you'll always fall short as an ally. You have to acknowledge the times you've oppressed Black women. If you believe you've never oppressed us, rethink that. Every white person has either actively or passively exhibited some sort of racism or white supremacy toward Black women. You're no exception.

At times, you'll harm us. You'll fail us. You'll never do this work perfectly. So don't expect perfection from yourself or anyone else. Learn from every mistake you make or you see another ally make. Remember to record these situations in your journal. Revisit them to solidify what you've learned and help you become a better teacher. Remember, part of your journey is bringing along other white people with you. *How will you work on your harm with an affinity group or accountability partner? How will you begin?*

REINFORCE YOUR KNOWLEDGE

Use your journal to answer the following questions and discuss how you completed the actions.

Scenario

Your friends, one white (Michelle) and one Black (Pamela), are arguing because Michelle asked Pamela why she's always angry. Pamela tells her to stop stereotyping Black women. Michelle becomes defensive and says she didn't intend any harm by her comment. She complains that Pamela always brings up race and she's tired of it. Pamela tells her to save her white tears, which makes Michelle even more upset. What would you say at this moment? How would you engage both friends? How would you educate Michelle and also support Pamela?

Question 1: Why is it important to acknowledge the harm you've caused a Black woman? How does that help you as an ally?

Question 2: How will you work through the process of making amends to a Black woman? What are the steps? What do you hope to learn?

Action

Find a short article, podcast, documentary, or video about racism and Black women. What is the title? What did you learn from it about what we experience? What did you learn about yourself while watching or reading it?

Chapter 5

EVENING THE ODDS

Recognizing how you benefit from white privilege

White privilege means white people have inherent advantages based solely on their skin color. From birth, you enjoy certain rights Black people don't. You haven't earned these benefits, and you don't question them. You just go about your life knowing—and you do know—that your life is decidedly easier than a Black person's life.

White privilege doesn't mean you're wealthy. It doesn't mean your life is easy. It means your skin color affords you certain advantages over Black people. *Do you accept that you have white privilege? If so, how have you benefited? If not, what would prove it to you? (This is a time to check in with your accountability partners or pose the question in a group.)*

White privilege has been studied and researched. Yet too many white people refuse to acknowledge its existence. They claim to have no advantages. They say they've accomplished what they set out to do simply through hard work. The assumption is that Black people don't work hard enough. We're lagging behind because we don't have the same drive and work ethic as white people. *Have you ever heard or*

believed Black people don't work as hard as white people? What are some reasons white people say this? This is patently untrue. It's frustrating to produce evidence of white privilege just for a white person to dismiss it. Instead, when I speak to white people who say they're not racists, I ask them if they believe they have white privilege. While more white liberals seem to understand how their skin color helps them through life, many still deny that their whiteness has anything to do with their successes in life. Let's look at a few examples of white privilege. I challenge you to remain open-minded and keep your defenses in check while you go through this chapter. Don't allow your ego to let you deny your privilege. ***How does denying white privilege affect your journey as an ally?***

I wanted to share a report by the Armed Conflict Location & Event Data Project (ACLED) that showed the correlation between BLM protests and violence—whether that violence came from white supremacist groups or law enforcement. In 2020, ACLED recorded more than 10,500 demonstrations between May 24 and August 22. Of these demonstrations, over 80% had some connection to BLM. Out of that number, only 5% turned violent. The report stated that BLM protests were overwhelmingly peaceful. However, in a more recent poll, 42% of respondents still believed that protestors' main goals included violence and destruction. ***Why do people believe BLM is violent when there's overwhelming proof to the contrary? How does this support white privilege?*** Even though these protests were mostly peaceful, more than 9% of protests were met with government intervention compared to only 3% of all other demonstrations. This was also an increase from July 2019, when government intervention was under 2% for all demonstrations.

White people simply don't like when Black people protest racism. History lessons don't teach us how white people felt about Dr. Martin Luther King, Jr., during his time. It might surprise you to know that white people saw him as a troublemaker. Yet Dr. King led exclusively non-violent protests. Any violence occurred at the hands of white people and law enforcement. *How does white privilege factor into white people not supporting Dr. King?* Like modern-day activists, he was told to give the country time to make the needed changes so Black people could achieve equality. It's a privileged position for white people to ask us, generation after generation, to wait for the very rights they freely enjoy. Dr. King's actions were instrumental in the passage of the Voting Rights Act of 1965. BLM protesters not only fight for police reform but also were instrumental in signing up voters during the 2020 election. Republicans continue to try to strike down these protections for Black voters. Even today, we encounter voter suppression. *What do you know about modern-day voter suppression?* We're still on the receiving end of police violence. Yet we're asked to keep waiting for equality. We're told these things take time. White people complain that we're impatient and we exaggerate the impact of racism on our everyday lives. They refuse to put themselves in our place. The idea that they could be murdered by the police or prevented from voting simply because of the color of their skin never crosses their minds. *What would you do if you were blatantly prevented from voting?* White privilege tells them they will never face these challenges. White privilege allows them to ignore any issues that don't directly affect them. That's why allies must not only sympathize with our struggles. They also must actively fight with us to defeat the oppression Black people endure.

Consider what happened in our country just weeks before President Joe Biden took office. On January 6, 2021, Trump supporters assaulted Capitol police officers and broke into the Capitol building. Police officers were immediately overpowered. Many of them were injured, and one officer even died that day. Rioters also died. The assault on the police went on for hours, with rioters chanting "Hang Mike Pence" as they broke down doors looking for him. They also yelled for violence against Speaker of the House Nancy Pelosi if they found her. Videos showed senators and staffers running out of the Senate chamber to safety while others took cover in offices.

Later on we heard from people hiding in the building about what they saw and heard. From their accounts, many believed they would die that day. Yet when the situation was finally under control and the building secured, rioters were allowed to just go home. They weren't arrested. Even later on, when arrests began, these violent white supremacists were given permission to take vacations and post bail. These insurrectionists would have murdered senators, staff, and any other Capitol building workers if they had been able to find them. Yet most of them remain in the comfort of their own homes. One woman had planned a trip to Mexico, and the judge allowed her to go. That's white privilege. ***How do you think Black people in the Capitol that day felt?***

I've watched the videos of those riots many times. The

Capitol police were obviously outnumbered and ill-equipped to handle the insurrectionists. Now contrast that with a planned peaceful protest by BLM in Washington, D.C., in June 2020. Those pictures are a stark reminder of the privilege white people have even when they loudly state their purpose is to commit violent acts. The image I remember most from the BLM protest in Washington, D.C., are the rows and rows of National Guardsmen in full riot gear standing on the steps of the Lincoln Memorial, waiting for these protesters to arrive. We know what happens when Black people protest against police brutality and/or for the equality of Black people. The riot police come out. We're beaten and arrested. We aren't treated like human beings. We're not allowed to just leave the premises. We're *forced* to leave. Police attack us with batons, guns, and tear gas. This is what we encounter when we peacefully protest. About a month before the Capital riots, a large group of white supremacists were marching through Washington, D.C. They vandalized buildings and cars and attacked people in the streets. They tore Black Lives Matter banners off churches and burned them. What was missing during that violence? A well-armed police presence confronting and arresting rioters. This group was allowed to terrorize the residents of that community without any pushback from law enforcement. That's white privilege. It's also racism and white supremacy.

Let's move away from politics and talk about everyday white privilege that white people may not realize they have. Privilege that's focused on making your life easier is something you take for granted. These conveniences are part of a seamless, white-centered system that considers your comfort as a white person first. I'll give you an example. I rip my pantyhose on the way to work and stop at the local drugstore to buy another pair. The odds are nearly zero that I'll find nude pantyhose to match my medium-brown complexion. That's because most manufacturers created the color "nude" to match white skin, and local drugstores usually don't carry any other colors. They don't even consider that their non-white customers might come in looking for their shade. *Have you ever considered why flesh-tone colors are always based on whiteness? What other goods can you think of that base their color on white skin?* When this happens, the best I can do is go without—which I've done many times—or choose black ones.

Let's talk about bandages. They're beige to match white skin. When I cut myself and grab a bandage, it's obvious I'm injured. White people have the privilege of purchasing bandages that allow them to hide their wounds. This deference to whiteness by manufacturers is rampant in our society. Companies are just now coming out with some darker choices for non-white people. Purely from a business standpoint, it makes little sense that any product meant to cover the skin wouldn't be available in a variety of colors. Personally, I would feel like these manufacturers actually see me, and they would get my business. If they produced more color choices, I wouldn't feel like I have to either purchase the products made for white people or go without. *How could you as an ally push for more inclusive products in the stores in your community?*

Hair is another area in which white privilege rears its head. I change my hairstyles almost every month. Many Black women do. We consider our hair a part of our personalities, and we enjoy having fun with it. That's why you see us with every type of look, color, style, and cut. We wear it kinky, curly, and straight—sometimes all in one week. Black women's hair has come a long way in just the past ten years. The Natural Hair Movement has given us the freedom to choose whether to straighten our coils or wear them in their normal state. It's freeing to have our unstraightened hair more accepted. However, I would be lying if I said everyone was on board with this movement. Black women's hair is highly policed in the workplace. In fact, organizations have even created rules specifically for Black hair. They say employees' hair must be "neat." *Describe how you feel about Black women's hair.* Human resources states that no dreadlocks or braids are allowed because they're messy. In other words, Black women must conform to European standards of beauty. White people demand we assimilate.

Oftentimes this means that, for us, straight hair is the only acceptable look at work. *As a white person, I want you to imagine how it would feel if your manager told you that the way your head naturally grew out of your head was unacceptable.* My kinky, coarse hair must be tamed if I'm employed there. I must conform if I want any chance of future promotions. While other workplaces may not have a written policy, Black women are still discriminated against for how we present ourselves in the workplace. We're not allowed to wear our hair too "ethnic." We can't be too Black at work. Our cornrows, braids, and locs aren't welcome there. But our hair—our glory—has nothing to do with our intelligence, competence, or ability to do our jobs. Yet white people have made it plain how they view these hairstyles. They're unprofessional and unaccept-able. White people have created another way to control Black-ness—by telling us even our hair isn't good enough for them. Black hair has even been litigated, and not much has changed. We can't deviate from these rules. If we do, we're lessening our chances of success within that organization. **How is this white privilege? How does this oppress Black women?**

Let's talk about education. I grew up in a small, midwestern town. I loved school, and I was a good student. I graduated high school with mostly A's, so I had no doubt I would go on to college and that I belonged there. I didn't think about how white people would see me in those classrooms and lecture halls. I just knew I wanted to attend college, never considering that some of my professors would all but say they didn't want me there. My junior year, I took a "Women in the Media" class. I was a journalism major and wanted to understand what my role would be in my profession. An older white woman taught the class. The students were all white except for me and another Black female student. **How would you feel if in every class you attended, you were one of only a handful of white people? What if everyone else were Black?**

I immediately knew something was wrong, although I didn't want to yet admit this white woman was racist. Any time either myself or the other Black student raised our hands, the instructor rarely called on us. When she did, she made dispar-aging and rude remarks. She treated us like our very presence was a waste of her time. She seemed annoyed we were even taking her class. It wasn't my first time encountering racist teachers, but I thought college would be different. I was wrong.

A few weeks into the semester, she was giving a lecture, and affirmative action came up. I don't remember the context, but she was against it, saying, "Affirmative action isn't fair. No one should need that kind of help." I knew she was talking about the only two Black students in class—my friend and me. *Why would the professor make this statement? How would you feel if I told you that racist teachers are common at every level of education?* The classroom got quiet. Then a white male student turned to me and asked loudly, "How did *you* get into this school?" I responded, "I graduated in the top 10% of my senior class. How did *you* get here?" He glared at me and said nothing. I looked up at the instructor. She was smirking as if she had accomplished something. Maybe she wanted to embarrass me. It didn't work, but I had her number for the rest of the semester. I did my work. Other than that, I didn't raise my hand anymore in class. *How does this story make you feel? What could you have said as my ally in that situation?* White people have the privilege of others not assuming they can only attend college or win a promotion through affirmative action. The white student who asked me that question never considered that maybe I was a better student than he was. And I was.

I wish the story ended there. The other Black student and I became close friends throughout the semester. She and I bonded over the blatant racism we were experiencing in class. We agreed that we just needed to finish the semester. One day, the instructor was returning research papers to us. She walked over to my friend's desk, slammed her paper down on the desk, and said, "You plagiarized your paper. I'm expelling you. Get your things and leave." She turned around and walked back up to the front of the room. My friend sat there stunned. She said she hadn't plagiarized. I believed her, only because I knew this woman wanted nothing more than to see us fail. The instructor again told her to leave. My friend packed up her books and walked out the door. I heard her sobbing as she left. I saw her a few weeks later, and she had been expelled from the class. You might say she deserved what she got if she cheated. **How would you feel about the encounter if you knew for a fact she hadn't cheated?** However, the professor had no reason to call her out in front of the entire class unless her goal was to humiliate her. Otherwise, she would have asked her to come to her office. Her racism that entire semester culminated in an encounter I've never forgotten. I'm sure my friend hasn't either. **How can we teach white students to spot racism from authority figures in the classroom and support their Black classmates?**

Black people face many challenges in higher education. Representation is one of them. I saw only a handful of Black instructors in college, and I can remember only two Black female professors. As an adult who has worked in higher education, I know it's a widespread problem. For example, if a Black female student wants to study engineering, there's a good chance she will be one of the few Black students in that program at her university. She may even be the *only* Black student. **What challenges does this student face? How can white students in the program be an ally to her?**

The challenge comes when she needs support. One of the most important relationships a student forms in college is with their academic advisor. If you're in a program where there are few Black people, there's little chance your advisor will be Black. The odds are high you'll face racism and discrimination in that program—whether it be from professors or other students. Black students won't feel comfortable discussing their feelings of isolation or talking about their experiences with a white advisor. That's because a white person can't understand what they're going through. Plus there's the fear that those concerns about racism could come back to bite them later. Black students graduate from these programs in low numbers—not because they can't do the work but because there's no one there who looks like them to whom they can confide. They have no real advocates, and four-plus years in that environment is just too much for them to handle. *What challenges do Black students face in programs with little or no Black representation?*

Consider how that feels. You're the only Black person in almost all of your classes. You have no Black professors. How do you survive that? White people have little experience with being the minority. They're uncomfortable in those environments. Years ago, I went to a Black-owned restaurant in Los Angeles with a friend of mine. It was crowded, so we had to wait for a table. As we were chatting, I noticed two white men standing nearby. They looked terrified. They obviously weren't used to being the minority anywhere and were unsettled by it. I looked around to see if anyone was staring at them or asking why they were there (the reactions Black people often receive in white spaces). No one paid them any attention.

White people rarely have to feel like they don't belong. Even in the example I gave, this was one evening when these men were out of the comfort of whiteness. It's nothing

97

compared to Black people. We can't even be our authentic selves in these majority-white spaces without someone questioning us. White people take for granted that they will have plenty of representation wherever they go. They don't have to reconsider their hairstyle or brace themselves for the barrage of microaggressions they will inevitably face from white coworkers. White parents don't think about the harm they may cause their child when they send them to a school where almost no one looks like them. White people don't have to consider the pros and cons of moving into a neighborhood where they're the only white family. Black people must think about these scenarios and decide if the risk of harm is worth the job, the school, or the house. At the college level, Black students at mostly white universities must focus on their studies and try not to let the potentially toxic environment affect them. I'm not saying that white advisors aren't good at their jobs. However, white people rarely experience being the minority. They have no frame of reference. *How can white people in academia become allies to Black students?* Consider how these students feel in educational programs where they face marginalization, microaggressions, and isolation. Even when they graduate, they probably will enter workplaces with very few Black faces. White people have the privilege of deciding whether they want to work in an environment where everyone looks like them. Most Black people do not. We take positions in jobs based on our skill set just like you. Many times, those jobs are in organizations where we're underrepresented or not represented at all. We see few if any coworkers who look like us and even more rarely see anyone in executive positions. There's no one there to protect us, and white people have a hard time even believing we *need* protecting. *Why would Black people need protecting in pre-dominantly white organizations?*

Let's talk politics. Barack Obama became this country's first Black president. Eight years later, Kamala Harris became the first Black female vice president. While white liberals cheered for Barack Obama and Kamala Harris, Black people rejoiced and said, "It's about time we had someone who can speak for us." I cried when Joe Biden and she won. I didn't think I would ever see a Black woman anywhere near the Oval Office in my lifetime. Now I even dare to hope that before I die, I'll see a woman—a Black woman—as President of the United States. I'm excited about the prospect, but I'm also terrified. Many white people hated President Obama. He regularly received death threats, and the Republican Party threw up every roadblock they could, preventing him from achieving many of his goals in the eight years he was in office. During the campaign season leading up to the 2016 election, Black people witnessed the vitriol of white racist Americans clamoring to boost Donald Trump as their white savior and tear down Hillary Clinton. *How has your white privilege prevented you from becoming a target for white supremacists?* During his four years in office, Trump systematically tried to rescind any laws President Obama passed to help Black people achieve equality. I watched as violence against us and other people of color increased. I listened as white people became more emboldened. It reminded me of accounts I've read of how white people boldly accosted Black people during

99

the Jim Crow era. Even now, they publicly threaten us and other people of color. They eagerly follow the lead of Trump and brag about their affiliations with white nationalist groups. *How can you use your privilege to fight racism?*

Now that Vice President Harris is second in command and a likely future presidential candidate, I worry how white people will respond if she wins. The white-lash following Barack Obama's presidency was violent and terrifying. What will happen when a Black woman takes office? Out of forty-six presidents, only one has been Black and none have been women. It's time for a female president, and it very well could be Vice President Harris. While many white liberals cheer on this prospect, Black America worries about the ramifications of her presidency. *How can white people support Black candidates running for office? How can you use your white privilege?* Donald Trump publicly aligned himself with white supremacists and downplayed any violence against Black people. After the murder of George Floyd, Trump stated that more white people were killed by police than Black people. With those words, he gave racists permission to ignore police brutality against us while also giving them permission to continue their racial violence. White people are privileged to have mostly white people running this country. We've had one Black president. In the Senate's 232-year history, it's had only eleven Black members. Kamala Harris was the only Black female senator. As of now, Black women have no representation there. *What do Black women lose with no representation in the Senate?* Black people can't take for granted that there will be people making policy and passing laws who personally understand the issues that are important to our community. While white people can sympathize with us, we need Black people who know firsthand what it's like for us in this country. White people have the privilege of seeing a sea of white faces in politics. They don't face the uncertainty of whether the person representing their state, city, or community even acknowledges them, let alone is willing to fight for them. White people exist in every aspect and at every level of politics. White voters have the privilege of easily finding politicians who won't ignore them or further marginalize them. They don't have to consider our reality, where too many elected officials care little about the Black community because no one is making them care. **How can you as an ally work to elect more Black female politicians?**

Proving ourselves worthy of occupying white spaces is nothing new for Black people. Before we have the chance, even our names can prevent us from getting the position. White people assume certain characteristics about Black people based on those names. If it's too "Black," human resources might pass over that applicant in favor of a more white-sounding candidate. It doesn't matter if both candidates are equally qualified. How would we ever know we were discriminated against based on a name? Aaliyah doesn't get the interview for the job, but Charlotte sure does. **Why do white people judge Black people based on their names?** White people don't consider the arbitrary nature of these decisions. A name should have nothing to do with your decision whether to hire us. There's no correlation between our name and our intelligence. Yet again, white people have the privilege of associating names such as Sara, Tyler, Abigail, or Cody with higher intelligence when compared to Ebony, DeAndre, Shanice, or Kevon. Black parents know how white people perceive the unique names they give their children. For that reason, they sometimes avoid giving them the name they love. Instead, they call them something that won't hold them back. ***Do white people have to think about what they name their children? How is this a form of white privilege?*** It's another way whiteness tries to oppress us. White people even police our names.

Countless times over my career, I've been called the name of another Black woman at work. I'm aware of studies that report how most people have a hard time telling apart people of other races. While that might be true if there are many people of the same race working in an office, what's the reason behind this happening when there are only a few of us and we look nothing alike? For example, in my twenties, I worked in a small office with about twenty-five people. Four of us were Black women. None of us looked alike. However, the receptionist and I regularly were called each other's names. Now, I'm five-foot-five with medium-brown skin. At the time, I wore my hair short and straightened. The receptionist was five-foot-ten and wore her hair in various styles, including long braids. We were about the same skin tone, but that's where our physical similarities ended. Yet white people couldn't tell us apart. ***How would you feel in this situation?***

Years later, I worked for a large corporation. There were very few Black people and only two Black women on my floor. But you guessed it. She and I were mixed up on a regular basis.

There were several hundred white people on this floor, so you can imagine the difficulty of knowing all their names. The white people couldn't tell the difference between the only two Black women because they didn't care. *Have you ever mixed up Black people? When did it happen? How do you think they felt?* These instances have happened numerous times and in almost every job I've held. Even when I corrected these white people, most of them still called me by someone else's name. They understood their privilege enough to know that they wouldn't face any work-related consequences because they consistently got my name wrong. I wasn't in a position where they were concerned about making a bad impression with me. I didn't have any influence over their careers. It was easy for them not to see me as an individual. *How can white people pay more attention to these microaggressions?*

White people also have the privilege of regularly seeing themselves on the big screen. How would you feel if you rarely saw people who looked like you, and the times you did, they were relegated to a stereotyped sidekick, prostitute, maid, single mom, drug addict, or welfare queen? *Can you think of films in which Black women aren't portrayed as a stereotype? How hard was it to think of them?* While there are films that portray us in a more positive light, these aren't the norm. Hollywood is overwhelmingly white, and that probably won't change anytime soon. The Annenberg Inclusion Initiative conducted a ten-year study from 2007 to 2017, looking at representation in 1,100 popular films. They based their research on the number of characters with speaking roles. The study found that only 12.1% of those films had any Black speaking roles. This number hadn't changed in the ten years they conducted this research. Of the top 100 films of 2017, forty-three of them had no Black female speaking roles in them. *Why do you think these top filmmakers didn't use Black women in their films?* During the same period, they found that only 5.2%—or sixty-four—of the directors were Black. Only four directors were Black women. In 2017, only one Black female director was working on a major film. In that same year, Black characters in films increased 41.8% when a Black director led the film compared to films with no Black director. When Black directors took the lead, Black women made up 18.5% of characters with speaking roles compared to 2.5% of films with no Black directors. Looking at data from 2015 to 2017, they reported that in 2015, three of the 1,100 films had no white female speaking roles, and forty-eight had no Black female speaking roles. In 2016, the number of non-speaking roles for white females increased to eleven films. However, the number is far below the forty-seven films with no Black women speaking roles. In 2017, the numbers dipped in both groups—seven for white women and forty-three for Black women.[11]

When we Black people go to movies, we don't have the privilege of easily finding many characters who look like us and are written to show us as complex, multidimensional people with unique stories and experiences. Screenwriters produce numerous films portraying white people this way.

---

11   Smith, S. L., Choueiti, M., Pieper, K., Case, A. & Choi, A. (2018). Inequality in 1,100 popular films: Examining portrayals of gender, race/ethnicity, LGBT & disability from 2007 to 2017. http://assets. uscannenberg.org/docs/inequality-in-1100-popular-films.pdf

Black people have those same experiences. Yet movies that portray the diversity and richness of our lives rarely make it onto the big screen. Imagine looking for films to watch with people who looked like you. You notice the lack of representation in particular genres. **How would you feel?** It's lazy and unfair to constantly relegate us to roles that portray us as racial stereotypes. Filmmaking encompasses every experience imaginable. Yet for Black people, it reflects the same white privileged view that we're two-dimensional beings with not one interesting story to tell. So there's no reason to look for more meaningful ways to portray us on-screen. **Think of films you've seen that have Black characters. What types of roles did you see? What roles haven't you seen Black people portray?**

White people live in a white-centered world. Your comfort is prioritized. Your needs are put first. Your existence is considered above anyone else. Yet you deny and deflect the idea of white privilege as if you'll lose something if you admit that you benefit from it. If you fight the idea that your white skin gives you unfair advantages over Black people, you're missing out on an important lesson for allies. **What lesson do you miss? How does that affect you as an ally?** If you don't admit you have white privilege, you can't use it to fight for us. We'll delve more into that in later chapters, but for now, I want you to think about the power of that privilege. If you're struggling with seeing the advantages it gives you, ask other white people to help you learn and understand. Accepting your white privilege means you can then find ways to use that privilege in your ally work.

REINFORCE YOUR KNOWLEDGE

Use your journal to answer the following questions and discuss how you completed the actions.

Scenario

You work in a mostly white office. A Black woman has just been hired. She wears her hair in long dreadlocks. You're sitting at your desk and overhear two coworkers commenting on her hair. They say her hair looks dirty. What would you say to them? What actions would you take?

Question 1: How can white people be allies in the workplace? Using your white privilege, what are some steps you can take to support Black women there?

Question 2: How does your privilege factor into your daily life? How does it make your life easier?

Action

Visit your local drugstore or grocery store. Go to the ethnic hair section. Notice where it is located. Is it locked? Then go to the pantyhose section and take note of the colors available. Lastly, go to the hair color section. Is there Black hair color? Compare products marketed for white skin versus Black skin. What differences do you see? Discuss this with your affinity group or accountability partner.

Chapter 6

HOW WHITE WOMEN BETRAY US

Upholding your adjacency to white men supports white supremacy

The majority of white male voters supported Donald Trump in both the 2016 and 2020 presidential elections. Even with his blatant misogyny, racism, and the accusations of sexual assault, white female voters also overwhelmingly supported him. *How does supporting a candidate like this hurt women? How does it hurt Black women?* This doesn't surprise me. However, following every election cycle, pundits seem desperate to explain why white women vote like white men even though white men create and support laws and legislation to oppress them.

One reason always bubbles to the top: White women are victims and naively follow white men into not only supporting white supremacy but participating in oppressing other women. *When do you think this idea that women are victims of white men began?* The media pushes the narrative that white women are simply standing by their men, and white men are solely responsible for the hatred and oppression of Black people. And yet both support and protect white supremacy. White female Trump voters are also more likely to endorse sexist beliefs—a stance that disproportionately affects Black women, especially in the workplace. *What does their support of sexism tell you about these women?*

A 2018 study compared the likelihood of white women supporting sexism and its relationship to their voting habits. Researchers looked at the 2012 and 2016 presidential elections. *Were you shocked? How did you expect these women to vote, knowing what they did about Trump?* The study investigated whether their votes showed party loyalty or sexism. White women shocked pundits and observers with their support of Donald Trump, particularly during an election when Hillary Clinton became the first female nominee for either party. While Trump flaunted his attitudes about women, it didn't deter most white women who voted Republican. These women also weren't affected by any perceived gender-based equality. Researchers, using data from the American National Election Studies, found that low-income white women made up the majority of white women who voted for Trump. *Why do you think they were the majority?* In 2016, these women voted Republican in even greater numbers than in 2012. They weren't swayed by the blatant sexism Trump exhibited. These women overwhelmingly voted for Trump and in higher numbers than low-income white men. White women with no college degree also were more likely to vote for Trump. They supported "hostile sexism" while downplaying discrimination against women.

Even with all the evidence of Trump's sexism and misogyny, white female support of him never wavered. In fact, 88%

of them cast their vote for him and his beliefs, compared to 4% of Black women. Because white women have overwhelmingly voted Republican since the 1950s, these results shouldn't come as a surprise to anyone. *Why are white women overwhelmingly Republican?* Yet the media reported shock at the high percentage of white female Trump voters. They mistakenly assumed women shared liberal beliefs. This simply isn't true. Although the majority of all women have voted Democrat in every presidential election since the 1990s, most white women still loyally vote Republican. *How would you begin educating these women?*

The study then compares demographics between white men and white women who voted in the 2016 election. They found that education divided many of the voters. Forty-five percent of women voted for Clinton, while 29% voted for Trump. Fifty-seven percent of white women with college degrees voted for Clinton, compared to 29% of white women for Trump. *Why do you think education affects how white women vote?* White female Trump voters were more likely to be lower income, even more so than white men. Researchers concluded that Trump didn't mobilize working-class white men as much as he did white women in the same economic category. Not surprising, working-class white women also were more likely to vote for Trump than middle-class white women.

Researchers also discussed why Trump didn't lose white female voters because of his sexism. Their support looks like they're voting against their own beliefs. However, white women are part of the privileged class and understand their first-place standing among women. *How do you begin work-ing with white women who place their privilege above equal-ity for everyone else?* Poor white women who are dependent on their husbands vote Republican to keep their privileged status above non-white people. They support sexism and aren't concerned with gender-based inequality. These women place upholding their whiteness before their womanhood. They understand that their race gives them the most advan-tage in society. Nothing else matters.[12]

History downplays white women's support and protection of white supremacy. White women aren't stupid. Throughout history, they've shown us they're more than willing to partner with white men if it means they taste even a sliver of their power. *Why do white women side with white men—the very ones preventing them from enjoying equal rights? Why do many of them support causes that could protect them from the oppressive control of white men and give them more opportunities in life?* It's all about white supremacy and the hope that one day they will enjoy the same level of power white men possess. *Why would white women vote against their best interests when it hasn't earned them equality? What do they gain in preventing their own equality? How do they benefit by keeping white women subservient to white men?*

As a Black woman, I fight for my rights and the rights of all women. Oftentimes, you see Black women speaking up

---

12   Cassese, E. C. & Barnes, T. D. (2019). Reconciling sexism and women's support for Republican candidates: A look at gender, class, and whiteness in the 2012 and 2016 presidential races. *Political Behavior, 41*, 677–700. https://doi.org/10.1007/s11109-018-9468-2

against unfair systemic racism related to health care equality, education reform, workplace discrimination, and any other inequities we see that prevent us from having the same rights as white people. If you notice, our concerns are the same as every other American. By extension, white women benefit from the labor of Black women as we do the bulk of the work to fight oppression. *How do white women benefit from the labor of Black women fighting for equal rights?* While white women enjoy many of the perks of whiteness, they're still subjected to misogyny and sexism that objectify women and prevent them from achieving their goals. Black women have been on the forefront of the gender equality fight for generations. Even Gloria Steinem readily admits there would have been no feminist movement without Black women. However, white women continue to thwart our successes.

During the women's suffrage movement, white women tried to separate the needs of Black women from their own goals and achievements. Suffragettes weren't fighting for the rights of Black women. They focused solely on achieving voting rights for white women. White women were happy to put Black women on the back burner if it meant streamlining their movement and getting what they wanted without the added nuisance of racism. White suffragettes refused to acknowledge the strong connection between sexism and racism. *Why would white women ignore the relationship between them?* However, Black women recognized the connection early on. During suffrage marches, they were purposely kept out of the fold, segregated to march amongst themselves and not mix with the white suffragists. However, women like activist and journalist Ida B. Wells refused to be silenced. She continued to fight for voting rights with the understanding that racism was an integral component of that fight. She knew that one must be fought alongside the other. Today Black women still understand the connection between racism and sexism. The latter takes the pain of racism and adds to it the injustices we also experience as women. This includes the racial stereotypes that label us as promiscuous seductresses controlled by our own desires or welfare queens who are too lazy to work. *What stereotypes have you heard or said about Black women? How do these stereotypes negatively affect us?*

The Women of the Ku Klux Klan (WKKK) was formed toward the end of the women's suffrage movement. In fact, many of its founders were also suffragettes. *Why would white women be both suffragettes and members of a white supremacist group?* The WKKK is exactly what it sounds like—the women's branch of the KKK. This group supported the racist ideology of the main organization. Instead of forming a sisterhood with other members of the suffrage movement, they decided to align with a violent racist organization that allowed them to openly believe and say what they wanted. By some accounts, WKKK membership topped 250,000 white women, all happy to be part of a group whose foundation rested on racial hatred and oppression.[13]

---

13   Bragg, K. (2021, January 5). First came suffrage. Then came the Women of the Ku Klux Klan. *USA Today*. https://www.usatoday.com/story/news/nation/2021/01/05/suffrage-ties-women-ku-klux-klan-sociologist-says/4092728001/

Black women boldly entered white spaces such as the suffrage movement because they understood that the oppression they experienced would not only affect them but also future generations of Black women. From Harriet Tubman freeing slaves to current Black female leaders, that battle continues—and with the understanding that we simultaneously face sexism and racism. While Black women claim a sisterhood that nurtures our relationships with each other and encourages us to stand together, white women treat each other as competition. ***Why do white women compete with each other? What do they hope to gain?*** Over the years, white women in "Real Talk" have shared stories of just how cutthroat they can be with each other to get what they want. While Black women try to uplift each other, white women happily tear each other down if it means they get closer to the white patriarchy power structure.

Many of these white women perform these same white supremacist gymnastics when it comes to allyship. They are accustomed to seeing each other as a threat instead of forming relationships to make themselves stronger allies to us. So when we're mentoring white women about what allyship means, we also must confront them when they try to form any hierarchy amongst their ranks. White women regularly attempt to categorize other allies by how good they are as an ally, inevitably placing themselves at the top. This behavior is antithetical to what it means to be an ally and successfully performing anti-racist work. I've often stepped into conversations surrounding who is the best ally to Black women. I inform them that, while Black women pay attention to the effort allies put into the work, we know that at any given time, white women can fall right back into their racist ways. That's why we're hesitant to play the game of good allies versus bad allies. White women don't think about what collectively is best for them. If they did, they would realize that aligning themselves with Black women is the only way for them to achieve true equality. With that partnership, white women wouldn't want to focus their energy on upholding white supremacy. Instead, they would reach out to us and ask how we can work together for the rights of all women. They would seek an education on racism and white supremacy and want to use their privilege to fight the very institution they now protect.

White women fall into the trap of competing with each other in ways that only benefit white men. They adapt misogynistic beliefs that prevent women from getting ahead in the workplace. They take their cues from white men and support laws that prevent us from even having autonomy over our own bodies. They vote for legislation that punishes women struggling to feed their children and continually prevents us from achieving equality. While they sharpen their knives at each other, make no mistake that white men are taking note of their behavior to use against them. White men con white women into believing they're in this fight to protect the rights that others want to take away from them. If this were true, white women would already have all the benefits of whiteness, not just the scraps white men toss at them. However, white women must understand that embracing whiteness means oppressing Black people. Everything they enjoy because of their white skin further harms us. White supremacy forces us to navigate our lives in unnatural and toxic ways. We live in perpetual survival mode and pass down those survival skills to each generation in the hopes they live long enough to keep our legacies alive.

Yet white women stay silent and go along with the program of white supremacy if it means they have a shot at a piece of the white supremacist pie. It's how Trump landed in the Oval Office. It's how Brett Kavanaugh and Amy Coney Barrett gained seats on the U.S. Supreme Court. Otherwise, it makes no sense that white women would support white men who view them as second-class citizens incapable of making the right decisions about their bodies and their lives. *What do white women think they've won when they support white men trying to take away women's rights? How do they explain their choices?* White women are deluding themselves if they believe white men will one day reward them by giving them equal power. White men will *never* share power with anyone else other than other white men. Even then, they're stingy about what they're willing to give up.

White women aren't gullible. They aren't victims. Let's stop supporting the narrative that doesn't hold them accountable for their actions. They're throwing their support behind white supremacy, hoping it continues to win. We can't depend on most of them to suddenly decide that fighting for the rights of marginalized people means more than the slim possibility they'll share equal power with white men. Right now, they have their sights set on one objective, and until they realize that dream will never happen and the cost of those beliefs—the oppression of Black women, people of color and every other marginalized group—is too high a price to pay, they're disinterested in anything else. **Why do white women seek the power of white supremacy above all else? Why do they dismiss the importance of aligning themselves with Black women?**

Historically, white women have been right beside white men as they beat, tortured, and murdered Black people; prevented us from voting; and threatened us for trying to exercise our rights. Stephanie Jones-Rogers explains in her book, *They Were Her Property*, the role white women played during slavery. Historically, white women have been assigned passive roles when it came to buying, selling, and meting out corporeal punishment to slaves. We've been led to believe that, while their fathers, brothers, or husbands ran the plantations, the women ran the households. However, white women were in the very midst of slavery. They attended auctions and purchased slaves. They sold slaves and broke up families. They punished, and at times even murdered, them. White women were slave owners in their own right. It's a myth that they owned slaves solely through their husbands. Many of them ran plantations with the same cruelty and disregard for the lives of their human chattel. They made the decisions about punishments that maimed and killed slaves. They approved of whippings by their overseers. White women weren't swooning at the sight of such cruelty. They were willing participants and gladly took on those roles. **How do you view white women during slavery, knowing their active role in the institution?**

Fast forward to today, and we witnessed white women take part in the insurrection to overthrow the 2020 presidential election. We've seen videos of them determinedly marching toward the Capitol and participating in its breach. We saw them screaming at the top of their lungs that the election was stolen and Donald Trump was their real president. They readily joined in the chant to hang then-Vice President Mike Pence. During his campaign and presidency, Trump became the face of white supremacy, and white women followed him as if he were their messiah. They're loyal to Donald Trump in the hopes that one day he will reward them. He left office, and they're still waiting for his return.

It all comes back to what I said before: They want their payday. White women are holding their collective breath, wondering when they will be rewarded for showing their unwavering support to white patriarchy. But here's the thing: That day will never come. White men will continue their stranglehold on power until Black people and our allies finally break it. White women must understand they have no chance of an equal position within a white male-dominated power structure and that should never be their focus. White men won't accept them as equals, and white women who want to become allies to us must understand the ramifications for Black women when they align themselves with white men.

Why do white women dedicate themselves to remaining loyal to white men? They're power-adjacent, but they still have relatively little power compared to white men. Let's also be clear that white women have created this persona of being weak and helpless so white men believe they need rescuing and protecting. That's the leverage white women hope to use in their pursuit of power. I find it hard to believe white men would allow white women any power if they see them as weak and needy. So far, neither loyalty nor victimhood has earned white women a true place of power beside white men.

White men see white women as objects, as children who need controlling. It's the same way white people see Black people. The difference is they want to protect white women from the ills of society, one of them being the evil of Blackness. How many times have we witnessed white people using Black people as a shield for their own violence? Susan Smith claimed a Black man carjacked her and kidnapped her children when, in fact, she drove her car into a lake and drowned them. Charles Stuart claimed a Black man shot his wife to death during a carjacking when he had actually murdered her. A group of white men tortured and killed fourteen-year-old Emmitt Till after one of the men's wives said he flirted with her—a claim she recanted decades later. Amy Cooper encountered Christian Cooper, a Black man birdwatching in Central Park. After he asked her to leash her dog, she called 911 and lied, telling the dispatcher that he was accosting her. I could go on, but the point is white people use our Blackness against us to cover up their own crimes and show us they can get away with it. *Why do white people usually go unpunished when they exhibit violence toward Black people? Why do they perpetuate that violence?* White women have convinced themselves they need protecting from us, and white men have assumed the responsibility of keeping them safe. These grown women can't take care of themselves and make good decisions. So white men must step in and steer them in the right direction. White women hide behind white womanhood and white men readily take up the mantle of protecting them from us.

I wonder when white women will wake up and see that the white supremacy they protect so fervently is the very thing holding them back. **How would you begin educating these women?** Black women know there is strength in numbers, and we understand that fighting for a common cause can move us forward. White men also know this. Their loyalty to each other lands them on top and keeps them there. This isn't to say white men respect, or even like, each other. They simply have a common goal—to remain ahead of the rest of us by any means necessary. That means protecting white supremacy and white privilege. They're not sharing that top position with *any* women, including white women. **Why do white women want to remain part of a white supremacist society?**

Until now, we've had to rise up on our own with our current allies and hope that white women realize that supporting white supremacy means allowing white men to keep them in their place. Why? Because white supremacy and sexism go hand in hand. White men see white supremacy as a way to protect patriarchal hierarchies so men lead and women follow. Why would white women want this for themselves, their daughters, or any other women in their lives? They must wake up and understand they should fight for each other and for every other woman so we all have the same rights as white men. This power-adjacency to them will never get white women what they want. Black women understand that equality will happen only when *all* women fight for it. **Why aren't white women fighting with us? What prevents them from rejecting white supremacy in favor of the rights of all women?** White allies understand they can never align themselves with white people who consistently show they will continue to do everything in their power to oppress Black people. They know allyship means they fight against this white supremacist behavior so Black women can achieve equality. They understand that anything short of that decision means they're supporting racism and embracing white supremacy.

It's time white women stopped hoping white men see them as equals. They don't—just as white women don't see Black people as equals. Something has to change, and that something is the belief that white men will uplift white women in a way Black women cannot. Countless times, Black women have saved white women. We vote in record numbers to prevent white men from taking away our rights—and, consequently, their rights. **How would you discuss women's rights with a white woman set on aligning herself with white men?** Yet white women still believe a bigger prize awaits them. They've convinced themselves the position closest to power is the answer to all their prayers. **What do white women want that allows them to accept being relegated to second place? Why do they think so little of themselves and Black women, that they refuse to fight for equality alongside us?**

White women sabotage their own progress at every turn. Each time Black women destroy a wall preventing women from moving forward, a racist faction of white women unites with white men and attempts to rebuild an even stronger wall. It's obvious white women refuse to accept the fact that white men want to leave them exactly where they are—upholding a racist system permeated with sexism and misogyny that will never allow them equal footing to men. *Do white men treat white women as equals? Do they uplift white women and help ensure they have a fair chance at succeeding in life?* If white women put their own privilege aside for a minute, they can consider where women would be if we were afforded the same rights as men. That changes the game in a way that white supremacy simply cannot. However, that also means that white people fully support Black women's equal access to quality education, career choices, home ownership, and health care. Right now, we're subject to decisions in these institutions that have devastating effects on our lives. *How does equality with regard to hiring practices help women in historically male-dominated industries?* Recognize that disparity and it's easy to understand why Black women fight so hard for the very rights white people take for granted.

Think about the policies that prevent women from accessing low-cost health care screenings and contraception from clinics like Planned Parenthood. Yes, the same Planned Parenthood Republicans want us to believe just perform abortions. In reality, abortions make up only 3-5% of Planned Parenthood's services.[14] The remaining services

---

14   BeMiller, H. (2020, May 1). Fact check: Planned Parenthood abortion funding, business claim goes too far.' *USA Today.* https://www.usatoday.com/story/news/factcheck/2020/05/01/fact-check-wis-planned-parenthood-abortion-claim-goes-too-far/3057827001/

include access to birth control, pregnancy tests, prenatal care, STD screenings, and patient education. Clinics like this are important in communities because doctor visits are expensive, especially when you're uninsured or even under-insured. Some health insurance doesn't cover birth control, so women visit a low-cost clinic such as Planned Parent-hood to get health care they wouldn't otherwise be able to afford. Birth control isn't cheap. The Pill can cost up to fifty dollars a month. Low-cost clinics allow people access to quality health care without having to decide whether to pay their rent or receive medical treatment.

I can attest to the importance of these clinics because I used Planned Parenthood in my early twenties. I had uter-ine fibroids. Birth control pills helped alleviate the pain and regulate my menstrual cycles. I was underinsured and couldn't afford the medication on my own. I visited Planned Parenthood and used that clinic for the next three years until I had better insurance. The women who depend on free or reduced health services aren't lazy or stupid. This is what white privilege would like you to believe—that anyone accessing free or low-cost services is looking for a handout and not a hand up. However, these clinics *are* a hand up. They provide much-needed affordable health care so that people can pay their bills, feed their families, and keep their jobs. It's services like these that help many stay afloat. The women who visit clinics like Planned Parenthood work hard. They love their families. They do the best they can. Sometimes they need help. Sometimes we all need help. ***How do you feel about services like free clinics? What do white people*** *gain by not supporting services that help people when they need it the most? How do white people benefit when they do support these services?*

White people must recognize both your privilege and your own racism. These revelations are necessary for ally work. Discuss these concepts with your accountability partner or in your racial justice group and take notes on those discussions. *What do you recognize as white privilege? How do you acknowledge your own racism?* A 2012 study looked at white women who were part of an activist group. The researcher wanted to understand how they addressed their own white privilege and racism. Members of "White Women Against Racism" attended discussion groups to talk about racism and what tools they needed to fight it. They also explored their own racism and white privilege. *Why is this important in anti-racism work?* The study focused on how they worked through their whiteness, white privilege, and anti-racism. Twenty-one members took part in the study. They were observed in meetings and/or interviewed as part of the research.

When asked if they identified as racist, only one person rejected this title. Most participants understood that admitting to their own racism was an integral part of anti-racism work. Other participants said they admitted their own racism because there was this misconception that only people active in white supremacist groups were racists. *Why should white people admit they've exhibited racism?* One woman said calling herself racist freed her from the fear of being called one by someone else. Others said admitting their own racism made it easier for them to discuss racism with other white people. Many of them even went a step further, saying white people must admit their own racism before they can become anti-racist. ***What is the relationship between admitting your own racism and doing this work?*** One woman said denying your racism meant living in denial, and that denial prevented you from making any real change. Several people said acknowledging white privilege and working on your racism were two mandatory pieces of anti-racism work.

Several participants said racism regularly affected their lives and seeing POC friends experience racism indirectly impacted them. They also witnessed racism through the lens of all-white workplaces, the anger of POC, and staying aware of their own biases. ***Where have you seen racism?*** They believed that their responsibility to address racism was tied to their white privilege. One participant said she knows she can use her privilege for change. Another uses hers so other white people listen when she discusses racism. ***How does white privilege help you discuss racism with other white people?*** However, several participants did admit they struggled at times with seeing their privilege.

Other participants felt being women gave them some insight into racism. One woman conveyed her challenges with a white male manager. Another said, unlike white anti-racist women, white anti-racist men don't think about their physical safety. However, two female participants warned them that focusing too much on sexism might allow them to downplay their role as white people who perpetuate racism. ***What happens when white women equate sexism to racism?*** One participant admitted her feminism may have stopped her from seeing the intersection of race. She clarified this by saying many people believe feminists also understand racism.

White women know they benefit from white privilege. They know that whiteness allows them advantages and perks over Black people. That explains why they join white men in weaponizing that privilege against Black people. White women believe that, by keeping us in our place, it solidifies their adjacency to whom they believe reside at the center of power—white men. They don't care how much control they give away when they support white supremacy. They covet their spot next to white men and mistakenly believe they are valued for loyally staying by their side. If that were true, white men wouldn't require they accept less. White women go about their privileged lives not once thinking about what that unconditional devotion to the power of white men costs Black people, and it costs us in every aspect of our lives. It also costs white women in ways they refuse to admit. They've allowed themselves to believe the gains are worth the sacrifices. When white women make a pact with white men to uphold white supremacy, they not only cosign their approval of racism but also their acceptance of sexism and misogyny. They freely sign away the rights of women to keep their place of privilege.

REINFORCE YOUR KNOWLEDGE

Use your journal to answer the following questions and discuss how you completed the actions.

Scenario

You're a member of the white woman activist group described in this article. You're in a meeting discussing white privilege. One of the white women in the group gets angry and says she and her husband talk about racism and white privilege all the time. They both agree that while these things exist, they don't personally benefit from them. They also struggle financially. They've concluded that they have much less privilege than other white people and they're not racist. How would you respond? What resources would you give them?

Question 1: What would white women immediately gain if they began to recognize their own privilege and used it to fight white supremacy?

Question 2: How would you begin the journey of using your white privilege to fight for Black women?

Action

Start a discussion with your affinity group about why white people practice white supremacy. What are the benefits and how do those benefits affect Black women? How would Black women benefit if white women used their white privilege to fight against racism?

Part III

FROM COMPLICITY TO ACTION

· · · · · · · · · ·

Week 3

Chapter 7

WORDS AREN'T ENOUGH

Transitioning to real anti-racism work

By now you should have a solid grasp of what allyship means. You're regularly talking to other white allies to learn from their experiences and find additional resources for your library. Now it's time to use that knowledge to educate white people. It's okay to be nervous or scared. That's normal. Remember that your discomfort is a sign of growth. In this chapter, I'll provide you with some tips you can use before, during, and after these racial justice conversations. These tips can help you have more productive discussions and learn important lessons from these encounters. *What makes you most nervous when you think about educating another white person?*

Your journal already contains a wealth of information to assist you in educating others. One of the most persuasive tools you can use in these conversations will be your own experiences and insights. It's important to talk about your ongoing journey with allyship. Personalizing a discussion by including what you've learned about yourself and being an ally helps you connect with the other person and begin to form a level of trust. You never want to distance yourself from your own racism when you're trying to educate other white people. *What have you learned so far about your racism?* Don't come across like you're too good to make a mistake or that you've never made one (we'll discuss perfectionism in Chapter 10). Part of allyship is admitting your own missteps. You also accept that sometimes you'll fail in this role. Sometimes you'll harm us. However, part of educating other white people is telling your own stories—even the ones that are uncomfortable or embarrassing to share. *How do you feel about opening yourself up in this way?* One of the most important lessons you can convey to another white person is how you hold yourself accountable after these failings, learn from them and try to make better decisions in the future.

Another reason I want you always to keep a journal of your conversations and interactions is so you don't forget how you felt or behaved when you were called out on your racism. It's important not to forget where you were and how you felt as a new ally. *What's the biggest lesson you've learned about yourself so far?* You'll still experience these feelings years down the road, but you'll have a better idea of how to handle them when they arise. When you're brand-new to the work, it's more difficult to rein in those harmful behaviors if you're feeling attacked. The behavior you exhibited will be the same behavior you try to help other white people overcome. They might feel like you're picking on them. They'll get upset and defensive because, if you're saying they're racist, you're also saying they're a bad person. Calling someone a racist almost always elicits an emotional response from them. They will lash out. When they do, one way to respond is "We white people are born into a racist, white supremacist environment created by white people. Of course, we will take on racist behaviors and ignore racism right before our eyes. It's normal to us, and that's what we're fighting to change. We can't uplift a system that props us up and keeps everyone else down." It's important that they understand their part in a racist society and why they must change.

In addition to using your journal, make sure you do your research beforehand. Think about what you want to accomplish in this first conversation. Whatever goals you set for that discussion, make them attainable. Don't set yourself up for failure by hoping the other person quickly admits to their racism and eagerly wants to work on it. That might happen, but it's unlikely. *What are some reasonable expectations for your first conversation?* Stick to one or two goals at most. Focus on accomplishing them during your talk. Depending on how receptive the other person is in that initial discussion, you can continue these discussions and provide additional resources to educate them. That's why it's important to be able to back up your words with research. *How will you make sure you continue to learn and add to your resource library?*

This is where you talk to your affinity group or accountability partner. This is why you must join a group with other white people working to become allies. The number of resources available is endless. You'll be surprised at how much information you can find on racism, white supremacy, white privilege, and a myriad of other related topics. As you're adding to your library, make sure you're organizing it in a way that you can easily find what you need. *Take some time to*

131

look at your library and organize it. Visit your local library and ask them for help collecting resources, too. Use the Internet to find anti-racism information that organizations have provided on their websites. They include these resources for people like you, who are looking for ways to educate themselves and others about racism.

In addition to using books and articles, find some videos and podcasts. Explore every medium you can. Make sure you know what's in these materials so you can have a productive discussion when you're trying to educate someone. Have these resources readily available. At some point, you'll come across a white person who demands proof about some aspect of racism. Have your educational materials available for them. This takes practice. Don't get discouraged if you draw a blank when you're suddenly confronted by a racist white person. The more you stand up to other white people and try to educate them, the better you'll become at knowing what information works best and in which situation.

Don't start a planned conversation without having the appropriate resources available that you can share with the other person. ***How would you begin gathering resources for a racism discussion?*** Bring books (or at least recommendations), documentaries, articles, or any other resource you think will help educate them. Consider bringing an article you can read together or a documentary you can both watch. If you're talking to a family member who isn't computer literate, don't give them resources they need to find on the Internet. Print out articles for them and bring books they can read. You can also find videos they can watch. Make sure the resources you present or recommendations you give align with what the other person can consume. *Why is it important to provide resources compatible with the person you're educating?*

Let's say you plan to watch Ava DuVernay's documentary *13th* together. Before you begin, make sure you know what points in that documentary you want to discuss with the other person. You don't want to start by saying, "So what did you think?" That question won't yield answers to guide the conversation in a direction where you begin educating that person. You don't want to allow her to immediately discredit something that she's read or seen simply because your initial query allowed her to dismiss the entire subject. *Why is it important to think about the questions you'll ask beforehand?* Take an element of that content and discuss it. For example, tell her why the documentary is called *13th*. The title is taken from the Thirteenth Amendment, which states: "Neither slavery nor involuntary servitude, except as a punishment for crime whereof the party shall have been duly convicted, shall exist within the United States, or any place subject to their jurisdiction." The Thirteenth Amendment was supposed to guarantee slaves their freedom. Instead, Black men were arrested on flimsy charges and imprisoned for years so they could provide cheap labor to work farms and penal colonies. These false imprisonments allowed Southerners to replace the free labor they lost after slavery was abolished. To this day, prisons continue to carry on the legacy of slavery. Mass incarceration is a booming business in this country, and Black men make up the majority of inmates. They still provide cheap farm labor, including picking cotton under a blistering sun in the same manner their ancestors toiled. The whole point of the documentary is to allow viewers to understand the relationship between our criminal justice system and slavery. Afterward, you can broach the subject of race and base it on the documentary's themes. Sometimes this helps you ease into the conversation since you're analyzing something outside of your immediate relationship.

I also want you to practice what you'll say before the actual discussion. In "Real Talk," allies constantly run through scenarios with each other. They role-play different situations to learn the best ways to educate other white people about racism. *What would you hope to learn from role-playing?* Find another ally to help you before you have the actual conversation. Decide on a topic and tell them to make it difficult for you to teach them. They need to get defensive and angry. They need to throw up every roadblock they can think of so you can practice knocking them down. Don't let them take it easy on you. In real life, white people will do everything they can to end that conversation. You want to be ready to counter those protests, demands, and emotions.

There are a couple of reasons why I say practice beforehand. You want to make sure that you have enough resources and that the resources you choose are relevant to that conversation. You also want to know within those materials, what are the most important points you want to highlight during your talk? *Why is it important to know the main points of the resources you'll use?* You don't want to just hand them an article or a documentary and say, "Here. Watch/Read this." That's not how we educate white people about racism. Give them some idea of what the resource is about and also tell them what you learned from it. Make sure that you've taken advantage of whatever you're suggesting to the other person. You want to know what that resource is about and how someone would benefit from it.

Role-playing also builds your confidence for when you have the real discussions later. That's because you'll have a better grasp of what you want to say. You also won't stumble as much over your words. You want to come across as competent and knowledgeable. Find other white people who can help you put together your talking points. You'll gain valuable insights from running through various scenarios of your upcoming discussion. Also, take advantage of helping other white people with their own conversations. **Why is this important?** You can assist them in finding resources and deciding the best way to broach a topic. Volunteer to take part in scenarios where you're the white person resisting the information. You'll be surprised at how different it feels portraying the person who doesn't want to change once you yourself begin to change your way of thinking. Just because you're a new ally doesn't mean you are bereft of knowledge. You have information you can share from the lessons you've already learned in this handbook. **What's one lesson you've learned that you can share with another white person?**

When you're having an anti-racism discussion with a white person that you know, take advantage of the dynamics of your relationship with them. Whether they're a friend, family member, or coworker, how you discuss racism with them will depend on what you know about them and how they relate to you. Use that knowledge. *How can you use your relationship with another person to help prepare you for a talk about racism?* If your Aunt Natalie isn't much of a talker, try asking her questions about herself to make her comfortable. "Aunt Natalie, what was it like growing up here? Did you have Black friends? What do you think it was like for Black people growing up here?" Let her answers guide you toward the right time to introduce a discussion on racism. Remember to ask questions and listen carefully to the answers. You want to respond in a way that challenges them on their beliefs but still keeps them talking. *Why is it important to challenge them on their racism?* Ask them why they feel that way. Keep leading them back to their reasons why. Use the knowledge you've learned to counter their arguments. Make sure you have resources available to provide them with more information on that subject.

The odds are you'll need to work with a person multiple times. Don't compare your journey to other white people. Everyone responds differently to racism and the part they play in it. That's why you need a variety of educational tools. If one article about white privilege doesn't work, find another one. *In what situation would you need to find another article?* If the resources you gave that white person aren't getting through to them, go back to your library, ask your fellow allies, and do some additional research. You can then bring more materials for that person to study. The benefit of doing the work of discovering additional information is that you're educating other people while also educating yourself. *What is the benefit of educating yourself at the same time that you're having discussions about race?* In "Real Talk," the mentors work with many other white women to help them recognize their racism. These white women know that the conversations they have with other white women also help them continue their own journeys as allies. Although many of the mentors in my group have done anti-racism work for several years, they will be the first ones to say with every interaction, they learn more about themselves. In other words, they're continually working on their own racism while they work with other white people. Both are equally important.

I want you to refrain from starting a planned conversation in a confrontational manner. *What happens when we immediately argue with another person? How does it hinder the conversation?* You've had time to prepare how to begin this discussion. If you're trying to educate, beginning the talk with an argument won't work. Of course, arguments may arise during the discussion, but you never want to begin with disagreements. Talking about racism with other white people more often than not is a tough conversation at best. Even then, take a break and come back to the process. *What do we hope to achieve by taking a break during a hard conversation?* Arguing doesn't make for a good educational environment. However, let's say you're out somewhere and overhear another white person say something racist. Of course, your initial reaction will be to confront them. In some situations, confronting them is the best thing you can do. You want to immediately stop the harm they're causing with their hatred. *Why is it important to confront someone making racist comments?*

If a person is yelling racial slurs at a Black woman or they're online saying racist comments, your job at that moment is to shut it down. Call them out. Show up in that space for the Black woman being targeted. That white person might back off, but they might also come back with even worse racism. As you become a more seasoned ally, you'll realize who you can educate and who needs to be confronted and silenced because they're only there to perpetuate hatred. *What are some signs a person isn't willing to be educated?* They're not open to any discussion. That's why I tell allies: Don't think you'll change every white person's beliefs. In all honesty, it will be quite difficult for you to convince most white people to become allies. *Why do you think many white people don't become allies?* There will be people in the middle you've educated who will now think before they say something racist. They may try not to be racist. However, they will never be allies who are willing to fight racism. You can still try to educate people so they at least understand the devastating effect racism has on Black women. Down the road, they may decide to begin their own ally journey. Keep working on them. Your job is always to confront racism and try to educate others.

If you're educating someone in whom you are personally invested—like a parent or a sibling—emotions can run even higher. Because of the nature of these relationships, it's more likely that the conversation will become heated. When that happens, express to them how important anti-racism work is to you and why you want them to understand its importance, too. *How would you express your commitment to this work to another white person?* Explain that you just want to talk about their racism because you know it's hurting Black women. This is a good time to tell that person how committed you are to being anti-racist and an ally to Black women. Again, personalizing this conversation with your own stories and experiences will make it more powerful. You want to find a connection with the other person. **What are other reasons why it's important to personalize the discussion?** It could be the story of your journey as an ally. This is the time to be candid about your own racism and how you're fighting to overcome it.

This conversation is also an opportunity to be honest about your motivations behind your previous behavior and why you've chosen to think another way. Take advantage of the stories you hear from other white allies. One thing that I've learned in doing this work is that white people who are actively being allies will tell you every terrible story about themselves and their racist behavior. **What's the goal of sharing these stories?** They know that each white person who is doing anti-racism work has them. That's how you connect with other white people. That's how you get people to move over to your side. Remember, this work isn't about seeing yourself as better than other white people. It's about relating to them in some way. That's because you *were* them and, in many ways, you still *are*. Even if you've been doing this work for twenty years, you can always slide right back into racist behavior. **Why do white allies still choose racism at times?**

Before you begin your planned conversation about racism, lay some groundwork. Acknowledge that it's an uncomfortable topic. Think about how you struggled with that concept, too. That's exactly how they will feel. They will feel uncomfortable and defensive. They might get angry and cry. *How will that make you feel? How will you stay on track with the conversation?* Expect any of these reactions and acknowledge that it's an emotional topic when you see another person becoming upset. However, as part of their education, tell them that their level of discomfort right now is nothing compared to what Black women experience in this country simply because we're Black. You need to make those comparisons; otherwise, their emotions will win, and your attempt at educating will fail. The other person can be extremely upset and angry about the discussion but always go back to, "I see that you're angry. I hear it in your voice. However, how do you think Black women feel when they're marginalized and oppressed every day? Is our discomfort more important than that?" *Consistently bring the topic back to the work of fighting racism. What happens if you don't stay focused on educating?* The conversations will always be difficult. Just remember that you're there to provide resources to that person. Let them know that educating them is the primary focus of your discussion with them. You want them to be a better person. You want them to overcome their racism. Tell them you want to help them grow from that discomfort so that they understand the damage done by racism.

In Chapter 3, I talked about why it's important to find growth in your discomfort. *So far, how has discomfort helped you?* If you remain in a bubble where racism doesn't affect you, then there's no way for you to break out of those confines and actively fight for us. The ability to grow is an important part of allyship, but it's also an important part of being a good person. The discussion you're having with the other white person doesn't necessarily need to result in them beginning their own ally journey. They might not be ready for that. **What could be some reasons why they're not ready?** This discussion should focus on educating them about racism and the part white people play in that institution. Bring up whatever racist behaviors you've seen in that other person and try to relate them to your own growth process.

For example, your white friend asks this question: "Why are Black women so loud?" Have a response ready that talks about the stereotypical beliefs white people have about Black women and how they negatively affect us. Be ready to have a conversation that talks about all the other stereotypes that play into the angry Black woman trope. White people have called me "angry" my entire adult life. Even when I'm simply making a point, they accuse me of having a bad temper. It's also happened online, where no one can even hear my voice. If I'm going back and forth with a white person about an issue related to racism and I dare to push back on their incorrect assertions, they ask me why I'm getting angry. They tell me to calm down. This tone policing *does* make me angry because it's another way for white people not to listen when their white-centered views on racism are challenged. Instead of listening, they attack my emotions. **How does the angry Black woman trope affect Black women?** There are many resources you can use to begin and continue a discussion around stereotypes of Black women.

If you're having this conversation with a white woman, be

aware of some of the pitfalls that might arise. White women shouldn't compare their experiences to those of Black women. *Why do white women make comparisons?* Black women have the double oppression of being both Black and women. While white women do experience oppression, they also have white privilege. When white women are confronted with their racism, they oftentimes try to portray themselves as equally oppressed as Black women. It's simply a form of deflection. At that moment, they don't want to be seen as an oppressor. They want us to believe we're in a sisterhood where we're both fighting the same enemies. *How does this damage their support for Black women?* However, as discussed in Chapter 6, white women have proven themselves more than willing to stand beside white men and exhibit the same racism and white supremacy.

While reading this handbook, you might already have people in mind who can benefit from learning about racism. Now it's time to choose someone with whom to have that initial conversation. *Who will you choose and why?* When you're beginning this work, it's okay to have these discussions with someone you believe is more receptive to the message. She still might exhibit racist behavior and express problematic beliefs, but perhaps she's more open to speaking with you. I'm a huge fan of targeting what I call low-hanging fruit. If you have someone in mind you think you can more easily educate, go for it. *Describe the characteristics of a person you think would be open to an anti-racism education.*

Be aware that, when you're talking to people you consider "liberal," you might discover during your conversation that, despite their political leanings, they exhibit racist beliefs. Most of the people I try to educate are, in fact, white liberals. Don't let that label lull you into believing they're in any way anti-racist. Many of these people are practicing the same violent oppression as they uphold racism and wield their white supremacist beliefs. *Why do white liberals believe they aren't racists?* When I say "violent," I'm not just talking about physical violence. In August 2020, CNN reported about a group of angry white parents picketing outside a school because the school wanted to bus in Black and Brown students from surrounding neighborhoods. The "progressive" white parents didn't want the school integrated with these children. This didn't happen in the South, where so many white people mistakenly believe racism solely exists. This happened in Howard County, Maryland. This is what I call "white violence." *How is this school protest detrimental to the equality of Black people?*

These are the white liberals you'll encounter. They read about anti-racism. They say they support Black Lives Matter. However, in their day-to-day lives, these are the very people preventing Black people from progressing. These self-described liberals will fight against Black people moving into their neighborhoods. *How does this support racism?* They'll say a Black candidate isn't a good fit for their company. These words sound innocent enough. Yet their meaning is clear. These white liberals embrace systemic racism. While they support the idea of equal rights, they won't show up for us if they feel they will lose their place at the top. That includes the right to segregate their children into an all-white school, or drive into a Black neighborhood to receive a COVID-19 vaccine

143

even though they are well-aware that Black people have been devastated by the virus. ***Why do white people feel entitled to jump the line and get a vaccine?*** They're the very ones who will undervalue a property if they see Black people live there.

When you begin conversations with white liberals, find tools that talk specifically to how they oppress Black women. Perhaps you've witnessed microaggressions. White liberals are especially adept at these. Microaggressions are subtle ways white people invalidate us. It's how they discriminate against Black women. For example, white people tell me I don't sound "Black." I've heard this my entire life, and it took me years to understand the insult and racism behind those words. ***Have you ever heard or said this? How does this comment negatively affect Black people?*** They're saying that speaking grammatically correct means I talk like a white person. They're also saying that all Black people are alike, and I'm some kind of alien outlier. When white people come across someone "different," they respond in a way they believe is complimentary to us, when it's just the opposite. This could be an interesting conversation starter with someone you know is politically supportive of Black women but personally still stuck in their own racist beliefs. ***Why do white liberals also support racism? How do they benefit from it?*** Find a short video or article on microaggressions. Make sure you discuss the harm that comes from this behavior.

You may have heard white liberals brag that they don't see color. Perhaps you've said this yourself. If you have, you've also decided that stripping Black women of our Blackness and labeling us all as simply "human" solves the problem of race. You believe discussing race or racism actually makes it worse. Instead, you say we should be focusing on everyone simply as people. *What's wrong with saying we're all human beings without discussing race?* Somewhere in this speech, the word *unity* is usually thrown out, too. If you're talking to a white person about this topic, you could begin the conversation with a variety of resources about the women's suffrage movement, which purposely excluded Black women. You could discuss how the idea of unity has never included fighting for the rights of Black women. Find resources discussing health care disparities or how Black women are also at risk of police violence. Breonna Taylor, Sandra Bland, and Atatiana Jefferson aren't anomalies.

Some white people will even attempt to compare their struggles to Black people. They claim to have the same experiences in order to invalidate our challenges and downplay their privilege. They're not dismissing racism as a concept, but on a personal level, they're telling us that their lives are just as hard as ours. *Why would a white person say this when it's clearly untrue?* White liberals get just as upset as conservatives when you call them out. You'll see the same anger, defensiveness, and tears. My point is that it's okay to direct your education to people you believe are more receptive to talking about racism. I just don't want you to be surprised when the person you thought would be easily converted rejects your lesson outright.

If you get through to another white person and they choose to join you on your ally journey, that's a great boost to your confidence. We need those wins. It's what keeps us going. Just don't cut corners preparing because you think they will be easily swayed by your lessons. When I'm teaching in front of a class and have thoroughly prepared myself, I'm more relaxed and the message I'm trying to convey comes across more clearly and concisely. I'm not up there rambling because I didn't do my homework before I started talking. Even if you believe that person won't be difficult to convince, do the same amount of preparation before your discussion. **Why is this important?** Include what you already know about them. If this is someone who says they're an ally, then question them about it. Who gave them that title? What did they do to earn it? Remember that the term *ally* is a title *we* give *you*. It's not one you give yourself. Even after you finish this handbook, you shouldn't bestow that title upon yourself. Wait until one of us calls you an ally. You just need to focus on doing the work. **How will you stay focused on the work and not on the label of "ally"?**

While you're having these discussions, make sure neither you nor the other person is centering themselves. This is a common mistake new allies make. While you're sharing your own stories and providing information, don't focus the stories on how badly you feel about your past behavior. **What happens when you center yourself and your feelings?** This work isn't about the embarrassment or anger a white person feels about their racism. It's about how they can learn to do better and teach others to do the same. It's about how that racism has affected Black women. During an intense conversation, the other person may be overwhelmed with emotion. You have two choices: either get the conversation back on track or stop and continue when emotions aren't running so high. *What could happen if the conversation gets too emotional?* It's okay to step away when you realize that the education you hope to convey has been overtaken by anger. That's a perfect time to find resources on white fragility and how that behavior allows white supremacy and racial injustice to flourish. Talk about your difficulties with white fragility but emphasize how discomfort is part of the process every white person should accept if it means they help fight racial inequality. White fragility rears its head in various ways. One of those ways is actual tears (I discussed white tears in Chapter 4). White women specifically cry when confronted about racism because they want you to stop "attacking" them. You may see tears, too. Tell them you'll give them a minute to get themselves together. Don't allow their crying to scare you away from the work.

I also want you to consider your commonalities with the other person. If homeownership is important to you both, talk about the challenges Black people have when it comes to buying a house. During the 2006 real estate bubble, Black people were targeted by predatory loan officers. As a result, many defaulted on those loans and lost their homes. When discussing the educational system, there are many different topics where you can provide examples of the disparities between Black and white children. For example, a report by the National Women's Law Center found that Black girls were 5.5 times more likely to be expelled from school than white girls. It's not because Black girls have more disciplinary problems. There is a systemic issue with the way that authorities treat Black people in this country, and that trickles down to how schools treat Black girls and boys. **How does finding commonalities help your discussion with the other person?**

You'll come across many white people who refuse to change. These might include your family members and friends. Try to educate them anyway. Use the resources you have on hand to help them. However, when you come to the point where you realize they're not ready or willing to internalize what you're trying to teach them, it's okay to let that go. That doesn't mean you stop confronting them on their racism. It just means you pivot from being an educator to an agitator.

Anytime they say or do something racist, you call it out. **Why should you continue to confront their racism?** You become the person who is known for getting in everyone's faces when they exhibit racism. You're the one at Sunday dinner that they know will bring up the subject of racism and ask questions of family members about their actions or inactions.

After you finish your conversation, make sure you debrief with another white person. You want to learn from that discussion so you do better the next time. Check your ego. Open yourself up to constructive criticism that will help you become more effective during these discussions. Keep practicing and having real conversations, but don't forget to role-play any chance you get. That's how you keep getting better at confronting racism and fighting for us. **What questions would you ask when you're debriefing from your conversation?**

REINFORCE YOUR KNOWLEDGE

Use your journal to answer the following questions and discuss how you completed the actions.

Scenario

You're preparing a discussion with your cousin about the way he talks about his Black manager. He doesn't use racial slurs, but he constantly says she got the job because she's Black. He doesn't think she's qualified and doubts she even has the education and experience needed to do the job. Find three resources you'll bring to that discussion. Also, work with other allies and decide how you'll begin the conversation. What do you hope to achieve?

Question 1: What are some open-ended questions you can ask if you're discussing racism with a white person who doesn't like her child's teacher because she's Black?

Question 2: Name four ways you can prepare for your racism discussion with another white person.

Action

Role-play the above scenario with your accountability partner. How would you begin the conversation? How would you use the resources you found? What discussions can you have using these resources?

Chapter 8

FAMILY AND FRIENDS

Influencing and educating your inner circle

Black women deserve more than to be relegated to an afterthought, second to the intentions of white people. This will probably be one of the hardest lessons for you to learn. However, as an ally, you must continually remind the people you're educating that the impact of their words is always more important than the intention behind them. Remember this lesson when trying to change minds. Now let's get into how to influence people who are part of your inner circle. Your inner circle is comprised of anyone you know well and whom you trust—usually family and friends. While education might change their minds, a more mindful approach is needed when trying to influence them so they begin their own ally journey. While you're still educating people, you can help them stay on the path to learning about racism by using your own behavior and actions to make them think. Try to educate them using your resources; however, you'll also use a variety of other tools to influence their beliefs. *How will resources help you when you're trying to influence others?* Sometimes you'll give them materials. Other times you'll need to do more homework so you have a variety of resources to give them. It's easy to doubt yourself when the most influential people in your life ask why you're now different. When this happens, talk it through with your support system. This is a great situation to pose to your group, too. Most allies have encountered this pushback from the people closest to them. *Why do you think white people criticize anti-racism work?* See how they handled it and implement some of their tools into your own situation.

Part of leading by example includes diversifying your inner circle. If you claim to fight for Black women but don't personally know any of us, you're missing out on a vital part of your education as an ally. Having diverse friendships, which include Black women, not only helps you become a better ally, it also proves to your inner circle that you value us as a part of your life. *Why is it important to talk with Black women?* You may not have any Black women who live nearby, but you can find us in your online group. Show up in that space to support us and engage in conversations. Don't ask for free labor. That's not what I mean. Our entire existence doesn't revolve around discussing racism. Like you, we have lives, jobs, and families. Remember, the core parts of who we are are very similar to your own. *On what other topics would you want to connect with us?* We talk about our children and our relationships. We ask for advice on where to vacation, fix our car, or find good cuisine. Many women in "Real Talk" have formed close friendships with each other. Those friendships have not only diversified their inner circles but have also enhanced their lives because it's a relationship they both value. *How do you think this connection would person-ally benefit you? How would it help you with your ally work?* As those relationships deepen, they share more about each other and their struggles.

That's how you can support Black women—by standing behind our causes and taking the time to understand us as individuals. White people who have been allowed into our inner circles can't take that position for granted. *What should you do to show that you appreciate that level of trust?* We don't let just anybody close to us, and we're especially wary of white people. However, once we allow you a place in our lives, we expect you to listen and learn from us. If you need to find Black women, look around your community and neighborhood. See what organizations we're leading and join them to support our causes. Otherwise, find us online, fol-low us, and talk to us. *How would this relationship influence your inner circle?* This way, you're walking the walk. Your interactions with Black women will help you in your ally journey and let other white people know that you're serious about anti-racism. You're not here just for show. You're join-ing us to make real change. Share these valuable lessons with your inner circle so they learn how to support us and better understand our experiences as Black women.

You're responsible for the white people in your inner circle you're educating. If your mother or sister comes to you with questions, always make time to talk with them. If they need additional resources, provide them. Consider your inner circle part of your own affinity group. Keep hold-ing them accountable and pushing them. Like you, they must experience discomfort in order to grow. *Why should you keep working with them?* By calling them in when they misstep, you become their accountability partner. You don't have to tell them what that means right now, but check in with them. Discuss the circumstances of any mistakes and provide them with resources. Follow up with them to get their thoughts on the information you provided—and also to find out if they took advantage of those resources. Thank them for being open both to that knowledge and to discussions about it. Influence them by acknowledging that they listened to you. *Why do you think this acknowledgment is important to them?* They opened a door, even if it's only a crack. Step through that door often so you can continue educating them. Invite them to a museum exhibit related to Black history, an anti-racism discussion or even a film that talks about the Black experience. Otherwise, use the Internet to find videos of discussions on race that you can watch together. *How else can you keep the other person engaged with learning about racism?*

I also want you to lead by example and confront performative allies or people simply unwilling to do the work (I'll discuss performative allies in depth in Chapter 10). The people in your inner circle who are new to allyship will be tempted to fall into the trap of putting on a show for us. You must address this harmful behavior when you see it in them. In addition, your inner circle must see you address it in other white people. The longer you do this work, the more you'll be able to recognize people who want to be part of the racial justice arena but refuse to do the work needed to create real change.

This 2019 study will help put into perspective your role as an ally. It also explains the consequences of not taking the education and responsibilities seriously. Researchers reexamined interviews of twenty-two POC activists. The majority of people in the study stated white allies lacked follow-through. This contributed to the POC activists experiencing burnout. The study's participants, found through social media, identified as full-time activists who expressed at least one instance of burnout with their activism. They were asked open-ended questions so their answers and stories would contain more information researchers could use in their study. Although participants weren't asked specifically about whether white allies contributed to their burnout, it became a central theme in several of their responses. Participants said that they couldn't trust white allies nor their intentions. ***How does this make you feel? Why would these activists not trust the intentions of white allies?***

Out of the twenty-two participants, eighteen of them said the behaviors of white activists contributed to their burnout. They exhibited racist behavior and often sabotaged the work. ***Why would a white ally sabotage anti-racism work?*** They showed white fragility. When it was time for action, white activists refused to join the fight. They also took credit for other people's work. ***How does taking credit for our work harm us and our anti-racism goals?*** Thirteen participants out of the twenty-two said the "unevolved or racist views" of white activists caused them to burn out. They believed these white people didn't even understand the movement enough to contribute in any meaningful way. Working alongside them caused those participants emotional stress and exhaustion. *Why do you think these white activists didn't take the time to learn about racism?*

They also used their white privilege against POC activists. These white activists carried their racism right into the work and harmed the very people they claimed to support. *How does this harm Black women?* In addition to educating white people outside their organization, these activists had to expend additional energy educating white activists inside their organization, too. This was often met with resistance from these white people, who refused to do the internal work of addressing their own racism. *How can they begin the internal work needed to be a real ally?*

Other POC activists conveyed stories of white activists refusing to learn from them. These white people believed they knew more about racism than they actually did. One participant explained how white men behaved as if they didn't need to be educated. These men believed they automatically knew about racism *and* knew more about it than POC, many of whom studied racism. POC activists explained that white activists didn't view them as experts on the subject of racism. Instead, their lived experiences were downplayed or ignored. They were frustrated that the white activists didn't seek knowledge from the people who regularly experienced racism. *What does this tell you about these white activists? What do they need to internally address?* As I've said, understanding the theory of racism isn't enough. You must believe our stories and take action.

The study goes on to discuss participants seeing the very behavior in white allies these white people should avoid—defensiveness when they're given criticism. One participant stated that white activists have the privilege of not delving into the real issues of systemic racism. They could choose to disengage with no consequences. *How would you challenge another white person who isn't willing to seriously address racism?* One Black activist talked about a white activist who described their relationship as "friends," then used a racial slur when talking about him. Another participant stated her disappointment that a white activist who said all the right words about racial justice still showed herself to be a racist. *Why does this person remain a racist even though they've read a lot of anti-racism literature?*

Eight participants said white activists undermined them, stole their work, and invalidated them as POC. One participant noticed how white activists talked the most in meetings, to the detriment of the women of color present. *How does talking over people of color affect anti-racism work?* Participants expressed instances of white activists tone policing them. One person was even asked to control his emotions when he gave an impassioned response to an incident of racism involving a Black boy. *How does tone policing harm us?* Participants also talked about white activists undermining them and even lying to get ahead.

Nine participants said white activists' unwillingness to follow through and act caused them to burn out. These people mistook dialogue for action. *Why is this a danger-ous mindset?* They rarely acted on the knowledge they pos-sessed. While knowing is a good start, **doing** is what creates change. White activists also refused to become vulnerable in racial justice work. They didn't use their power and privilege to fight racism. They refused to take real risks. Participants explained how white activists chose not to be vulnerable to prevent any real self-examination of their own racism. *Why must allies be willing to examine their own racism?* These people liked the idea of racial justice work but didn't want to confront racial issues. *They* decided on the ways they wanted to engage, which didn't always align with racial justice work. *How does picking and choosing when you will act hurt anti-racism work?*

Eight participants stated that white activists exhibited white fragility. White people predictably retreated into whiteness and played the victim. When this happened, they took their focus off the work and centered their own feelings. Two WOC participants were labeled aggressive and angry by white activists simply because they possessed strong, asser-tive personalities. *Why are "aggressive" and "angry" labels harmful to Black women?* White activists didn't want to par-ticipate in the emotional, negative side of racial justice work. They wanted racial justice work always to make them feel good, and they expected POC activists to provide those pleas-ant feelings. *What is the problem with these expectations?* Participants said these white activists wanted the spotlight in the racial justice arena. They craved attention for their work, so much so that they took advantage of POC activists. They used their work without giving them credit. They aligned themselves with POC activists to give the impression they were serious about their part in the movement, even when that was far from the truth. **How would you address a white ally who isn't serious about anti-racist work?** These same activists also tried to silence POC by speaking over them or even speaking *for* them to show that they were, in fact, the real experts on racism. White activists even used the work of POC activists and attached their own names to that labor.[15]

The revelations in this study should trouble you. As an ally, you must address these toxic behaviors in other white people, including those in your inner circle. However, you should strive to influence the ones who clearly aren't doing the real work needed to be an anti-racist ally. **What tools would you use to influence them?** Their behaviors are actually hurting both the work and the Black women they claim to support. When you're participating in your group, pay attention to what other white people are saying and doing. If they're centering themselves, use your own experiences and resources you've collected to give them the tools to change that behavior. **How would begin this conversation with them?** If they're overstepping and talking over Black women, explain to them that silencing us only hurts the racial justice movement. Passing the mic (which I will explain more in

---

15   Gorski, P. C. & Erakat, N. (2019). Racism, whiteness, and burnout in anti-racism movements: How white racial justice activists elevate burnout in racial justice activists of color in the United States. *Ethnicities, 19*(5), 784–808. https://journals.sagepub.com/doi/full/10.1177/1468796819833871

Chapter 11) means you uplift our voices. You never replace our voices with your own. This is another important lesson to pass on to your inner circle. White people regularly try to speak for us. Numerous times I've confronted ones who try to explain my words to another white person, misquoting or misinterpreting my intentions along the way. This is never okay. Again, your intentions never outweigh the impact of your harmful actions.

Previously, I asked you to find documentaries for the white people you're educating to watch. Don't stop at just one. Continually suggest documentaries, films, and discussions they can watch. I also want you to add resources that directly address racism and its effects on Black people. These could be voter suppression, education inequality, racial profiling, employment discrimination—any topic that focuses on the oppression of Black people. If you can attend these discussions in person, make plans to do so. If not, find a live-streamed, online event you can watch together. Watching these events in real time is important because it emphasizes the urgency of the issue when you know the discussion is unfolding as you watch. You may be able to ask questions, too. *Why is it important to engage in these discussions?* That's a great way to get both you and the person you're trying to influence more involved in the issues being addressed. A good example of the power of social media is the grassroots efforts to engage volunteers during the 2020 election. Thousands of people became more involved and found ways to support the election from anywhere they lived. During every election, activist groups seek volunteers to assist them with canvassing, voter registration, and phone banking. *What other ways can you get directly involved?* This may not seem like a direct correlation to the issues Black people face, but consider if the 2020 election had a different outcome. You'll need to decide if this activity is something that will help influence your inner circle.

Your journal also contains powerful ways to influence people. Changing your beliefs and opening yourself up can be overwhelming for many people. *What have you already learned that you can use to influence others?* Talking about your own challenges and struggles tells white people in your inner circle that they're not alone in their feelings of uncertainty. Tell your stories. Use the questions I pose to you throughout this book to start conversations in which you can discuss your thoughts. If you need discussion questions to respond to a problem you want to address with another white person, query your accountability partner or ask people in your racial justice group. Crowdsourcing potential questions is a great way to get a variety of choices. Asking these targeted questions in response to a particular issue gives you a chance to influence that behavior by talking through it. Remember the guidelines I gave you about educating others. They're still in place here. Refrain from arguing, and always be open to listening.

Oftentimes, just listening can be a key factor in influencing others. *How do you influence people just by listening to them?* You won't change anyone's mind if you're interrupting them or shouting them down. "Real Talk" allies practice active listening, then address any racism they hear in the response. Think about what works for you when you're talking with other people. You want to be heard. You want to know that she's paying attention when you're talking. *What are some ways you can show her that you're actively listening?* It's tempting to mentally prepare what you want to say while she's still expressing herself. However, she will know that you're only half listening, and you'll lose her attention. Remember that respect during that conversation goes both ways. I'm not saying you should respect racist behavior, but it's your job to hold you both accountable to listen to each other. You must especially pay attention since you'll provide the guidance and education to help her understand and change her behavior. *What are some red flags that might come up for you during this conversation?*

Conversations should contain both give-and-take. If the person you're educating is loquacious, that's great. The more she talks, the more you'll learn about her. Use that information to influence her way of thinking. You might not have resources at that moment, but you do have the ability to discuss racism. You also can ask her to elaborate by saying, "Why do you believe that about Black women? Where did you hear it?" Then sit back and continue to actively listen. *How will listening and mentally taking notes of the conversation help you educate this person?* Your job is to challenge her. Ask her to explain the rationale behind her beliefs. This tactic is a great way to hold her accountable while also allowing her to consider the impact of her words.

Sometimes simplicity works best. Instead of thinking you must change your friend's entire mindset at one time, parse out how you want to work. Perhaps you want to start with white privilege. In a previous chapter, I gave you instructions to visit your local store to see how many different colors of pantyhose and bandages you find. Go on that field trip together. Don't tell them the reason why you're going. Simply invite them and walk down those aisles. ***What's the advantage of not telling them the reason for the trip?*** Begin a conversation about the lack of variety and see where it goes. This is one way to begin a discussion about white privilege. There are many from which to choose. For example, I've briefly touched upon the health care disparities between Black women and white women. You could discuss pregnancy mortality. Tennis star Serena Williams talked candidly about her own pregnancy complications. Even she encountered doctors who didn't listen to her, a situation faced by Black mothers that can lead to deadly consequences. There are several articles and videos you can use that discuss Serena's experience that illustrate the challenges pregnant Black women face when seeking medical attention.

Showing vulnerability also will go a long way toward influencing your inner circle. Share your own struggles with this work. ***What challenges can you share now?*** Allow the other person to become vulnerable, too. This doesn't mean they should center their feelings, but it's fine for them to say it's difficult to change or that they're struggling with a concept from the materials you provided them. Work together to overcome those obstacles so you can keep educating them. By now, you should have heard plenty of stories from other allies about their own challenges. Share those along with your own so the other person doesn't feel alone. *What stories have you heard that could help you influence others?*

Working with white women in "Real Talk" has shown me the importance of white people working together to keep each other on track. You don't want to quit. You also don't want anyone you're educating to give up. Try to influence them with stories of how you and other white allies have overcome your racist beliefs. Be honest with them and don't hold back. *What do you want to achieve by being forthcoming with your own racism?* This way of connecting with other white people will help them get outside of their own heads and do the work of fighting their own racism. That's the important part of this process. Focus on showing them that it's possible to be a different person. When explaining about the times you've felt vulnerable, make clear your own struggles and feelings about the ways you needed to change. Those embarrassing stories you hesitate to share? They're a powerful way to influence others.

Be honest with how much you wanted to change and the work you still need to do. *What are you still working on?* Discuss the times you failed to support Black women and how you did the work needed to improve your allyship. Don't sugarcoat any of your experiences. Tell them the vulnerability and defensiveness you feel when you're called out for racist behavior. Be honest about your own emotions. Explain that, while you might feel angry, you refuse to center yourself and your feelings. The work always comes first. Your feelings are just a symptom of your discomfort and desire to run away from some aspect of your education that you don't want to learn.

Intentions can also help you influence other white people. When I see people try to back away from their racist behavior by saying they didn't mean what they said or that it wasn't their intention to hurt me, I explain that, regardless of their intentions, they've still harmed me. It's like saying you drove too fast and didn't intend to hit someone in the crosswalk, killing them. Your intentions won't bring that person back to life. *How does centering your intentions affect how well you understand your words/actions?* You must address the impact, and that goes right back to being vulnerable and open to how your actions affected the other person. I'm not dismissing intent, but I'm saying that neither you nor anyone else should use it to decenter the harm you've caused. When you're educating others, you'll notice that centering feelings is the go-to deflection when white people don't want to confront what they've done. You've displayed the same behavior. *When have you centered your feelings during this process?* The difference is you now understand that making your good intentions the most important part of the situation means you've now relegated the harm you've caused to a mere casualty. Connecting on this level with other white people will help influence their way of thinking. Practice complete transparency when you're showing your own vulnerability. Work with your accountability partner and other white allies in your group to collect more examples of so-called good intentions and the potential for them to derail the work. *Name one situation in which someone voiced their good intentions to downplay their harm to you. How did it make you feel?*

Influencing others using your own stories and experiences

is a powerful way to create dialogue and begin educating other white people. The more you share about yourself and your own struggles, the better you'll get at knowing what parts of yourself resonate with another white person. Remember that not everyone will change. *What would prevent someone from changing?* You can have a variety of stories to tell them, and they won't budge. Know when to walk away. Use your time and energy on someone else. Sometimes you have to move on, hoping you at least planted a seed of knowledge that might grow in the future. *If someone doesn't change, what part of the education do you hope stays with them?* If you made them think about their actions, they might reach out to you in the future. Circle back with them later, but don't expend energy on people who aren't ready to listen. Your influence will only go so far. Not everyone will be moved by it or you.

Educating other white people and getting them to change is a battle that, more often than not, you'll lose. It's stressful and frustrating. As a white person, you have the privilege of stopping and retreating into your privileged life. Black people don't. The daily macro- and microaggressions are wearing, and it's no wonder we're exhausted by them. There's actually a name for this: racial battle fatigue. Racial battle fatigue means the stress we experience as we try to handle racial microaggressions. Every Black person experiences it, and it affects both our physical and mental health. I'll explain it with a study done with Black mothers living in a white suburb of Detroit.

The Black daughters of these Black mothers attended predominantly white schools. The researchers found that the women regularly experienced microaggressions from white parents, white teachers, and white administrators with whom they interacted at their daughters' schools. They fought these microaggressions using what the researcher called the "African American motherwork"—strategies Black mothers create to stand up for both themselves and their daughters. The study was framed using the idea of "the veil" (a term coined by W.E.B. Du Bois in *The Souls of Black Folk*), the invisible barrier that prevents equality between white people and Black people. "The veil" is meant to convey a space that protects Black people while we're inside it. However, once outside that cover, we're regularly exposed to racism and microaggressions. The study aimed to show the link between these encounters and racial battle fatigue, a phenomenon that affects us both mentally and physically. Black people also can experience headaches, stomachaches, fatigue, depression, anger, and resentment because of it.

Black mothers used three strategies to help their daughters have a successful experience in their mostly white schools: presence, imaging, and code-switching. A Black mother uses *presence* to ensure the school knows her main goal is to unconditionally support her daughter. She volunteers for school functions and plans how she will interact with school personnel so those interactions help her daughter. *Imaging* means she ensures her daughter sees positive Black female role models. She knows her daughter will be inundated with negative images of Black girls and women. This mother wants to ensure she sees the flip side. She wants to challenge those norms related to white standards. A Black mother also uses *code-switching* to teach her daughter to speak in a way that helps her succeed in white spaces. This hypervigilance shown by Black mothers leads to racial battle fatigue.[16] When you're fighting racism and using your influence on other white people, you're also pointing out and addressing these microaggressions such as the ones these Black mothers experienced. Racial battle fatigue is real, and fighting racism means understanding the heavy toll it places on Black people.

As Black women, we endure microaggressions on a daily basis. We're exhausted. That's why it's important that, when you're educating other white people about racism, you constantly look for ways to influence them, especially the ones in your inner circle. Pay attention to how they behave and address any racism you see. Take advantage of what you know about the people close to you and use it to your advantage. That knowledge will help you succeed in influencing their behavior and bring them closer to becoming allies themselves. Remember you're on a journey where educating yourself is a lifelong process. That also goes for your family and friends. There is always something for them to learn. Every chance you get, invite them to learn it together. That's how you influence real change and positively impact racial justice work.

16   Bailey-Fakhoury, C. & Mitchell, D. (2018). Living within the veil: How Black mothers with daughters attending predominantly white schools experience racial battle fatigue when combating racial microaggressions. *Du Bois Review: Social Science Research on Race*, *15*(2), 489–515. doi:10.1017/S1742058X1800022X

REINFORCE YOUR KNOWLEDGE

Use your journal to answer the following questions and discuss how you completed the actions.

Scenario

You're talking to a white friend about a new hire at their job, a Black woman in her mid-twenties. The friend states that the woman seems standoffish and doesn't talk much. She's told you that the office is mostly white, and she is one of only a few Black people. What do you say to your friend? How can you influence her to examine her opinions and think more carefully about these criticisms of her Black coworker?

Question 1: What tools can you use to influence someone who is well-versed in racial justice readings but still exhibits racism?

Question 2: What subtle influences can you use for someone in your inner circle who is resistant to educating themselves and changing?

Action

Create a detailed list of the top ten ways to influence other white people while doing racial justice work. Make sure you have examples. This list will come in handy when you're doing ally work.

Chapter 9

DON'T IGNORE RACE

Navigating friendships with Black women

I'm fortunate to have a small circle of white women I consider my friends. I trust them. They understand that, as a Black woman, I regularly face racism. These women are true allies. They jump in at a moment's notice to confront racists. *Why is this important when you befriend Black women?* They try to help other white people understand how their racism harms Black women. These friends are the ones who, without being asked, push back at racist relatives even when they know doing so could risk any future relationship with those family members. Fighting racism and white supremacy is one of the most important goals in their lives. They would never consider standing on the sidelines. They refuse to stay silent or be silenced when they encounter racism. *Why is it important that allies speak up, even at the risk of damaging important relationships?*

I've had both healthy and harmful friendships with white people. The harmful friendships involved white people whom I believed cared about me and by extension other Black people. I learned the painful lesson that white people are quite capable of forming a relationship with me while dismissing racism and actively despising my race. Cross-racial friendships should open your eyes. However, I see white people overstating the depth of those friendships. *Why do you think white people exaggerate friendships with Black women?* A friendship where you don't depend on each other or feel comfortable sharing intimate parts of your lives isn't truly a relationship that belongs in the category of friendship.

In 2016, researchers conducted a study of 1,055 mostly Black and white adults to find out how cross-racial friendships began and their impact on race relations. Seventy-three percent of participants were female; 55% of participants were white; and 32% were Black. They first delved into the nature of the friendships by asking a series of questions to find out the characteristics of that cross-racial friendship. Some of the topics included vacationing together, borrowing money, or socializing at each other's homes. *Why do you think researchers asked these types of questions? What does it say about the friendship if you take part in these activities?* Respondents were then asked questions about race relations. These included topics such as how societal messages influenced whether they sought friendships outside their own race or if they were comfortable being the only person of their race in social settings. Researchers also asked essay questions about these friendships. Topics included experiences that were upsetting, motivating, or inspiring. Researchers concluded that, while highly educated men were more likely to have a larger number of friends outside their race, women formed deeper connections in their cross-racial friendships. *Why would the relationships between women be deeper? What could you do to connect more deeply with a Black woman?* Participants were then divided into focus groups. Researchers wanted to find out the differences between same-race and cross-racial friendships as well as the social context, such as police violence against Black people. Respondents believed the stories of racism their friends shared but weren't comfortable discussing racism that became national news. *Why could this be a warning sign in the friendship? What does it say about the white person's commitment to that relationship?* They didn't want to misspeak and risk losing the friendship.

The level of trust, educational experience, and social value were further explored as participants responded with short answers. Some comments under "Level of trust" included:

A fifty-five-year-old Black woman said white people "don't get it" and stated the friendship would be different if her friend were Black. She added that white people "have a fear factor from segregating themselves based on old stereotypes."

A twenty-seven-year-old Black woman stated she had cross-racial friendships with many races and in the beginning, she might not have had the same conversations with white friends as she had with her Black friends. She added, "Over the course of time, as that trust started to build, the conversations became pretty much the same." *What do you think these white people did that allowed her to feel comfortable discussing difficult topics surrounding race?*

A forty-six-year-old white woman listening to others talk about cross-racial friendships said, "I have nothing to draw from. I don't really have any close friends of a different race."

A thirty-year-old white woman worked with a Black woman, and they both lived in the same neighborhood. Their husbands were also friends. "We talk about the struggles among races and we get down and dirty and it's so refreshing to just be able to talk about how we get past this." **What steps could they take to move these conversations toward actions?** Some comments under "Educational experiences" included:

A forty-six-year-old white woman said she tried to create movement in conversations with her non-white friends. She believed that the people involved in these discussions surrounding social issues must meet in the middle. **Do you agree with her assessment that we must meet in the middle? Why or why not?** She goes on to say, "The important thing right now is to at least be able to have the discussion. It might end up in a blowup, which doesn't intimidate me as much as it used to." **What is missing from her statement about conversations potentially ending in blowups?**

A thirty-three-year-old Black woman grew up in a diverse community with friends from different races. Once she attended an HBCU (Historical Black College and University), her diversity of friendships ended. After graduation, she worked in corporate America and had friends of many races. However, she said, ". . . it's just on the surface, it never goes deeper; you never have that conversation with people because you may not be comfortable digging too deep into that relationship." **How can her white and POC coworkers make her comfortable enough to form real friendships?**

Some comments under "Social value" included:

A forty-five-year-old Black man said, knowing the history

of how white people have treated Black people in this country, ". . . how I should forgive them and turn around and be friends with them?"

A forty-seven-year-old white man asked, "Why do I even have to have Black friends?"[17]

There are a few takeaways from this survey I want to point out. First, your friendships don't operate on the same level. You have friends who would be more accurately labeled as acquaintances. Perhaps you see each other at social events, but you've never socialized together. Maybe you've met for dinner a few times or gone on neighborhood walks. **What aspects of a deep friendship are missing when you're not confiding in each other?** If you're not sharing intimate details of your lives, then that's not the type of close friendship where you depend on each other or reach out when you need someone in which to confide. If you don't discuss those deeply personal parts of your life, you don't have a friendship where you're vested in each other's happiness, emotional well-being, and successes. That means, if your Black friend hasn't shared her experiences with racism, she doesn't see your relationship at the same level or connection as you do. **Why are Black women hesitant to share their stories with white friends?** Sharing our experiences is an emotional moment where we feel exposed. We feel vulnerable. If we can't trust you simply to listen and support us, we'll never allow you into those parts of our lives. Later in this

17   Plummer, D., Stone, R. T., Powell, L. & Allison, J. (2016). Patterns of adult cross-racial friendships: A context for understanding contemporary race relations. *Cultural Diversity and Ethnic Minority Psychology, 22*(4), 479–494. DOI:10.1037/cdp0000079

chapter, I'll discuss how you can deepen your friendship so you can be both a confidante and an ally to your Black friend.

At this point in your journey, it's time to discuss how your Black friend feels. Let her know you're open to learning, and that's why you're taking this serious step toward becoming an ally. Tell her that you're not expecting her to educate you. But if she chooses to share her stories, you'll believe her with no questions asked. *How does this benefit your friendship and your work as an ally?* Don't doubt her experiences or play devil's advocate. Doing so means you're more concerned with maintaining your racist beliefs than opening yourself up to the fact that those beliefs are wrong. If you're tempted to challenge her views on racism or ask whether her experiences were actually racism, you're exhibiting white supremacist views that will only hurt your friend. *How do you think she'll feel if you challenge her experiences?* Allies don't question or deny our experiences. They learn from our stories and use that knowledge to educate other white people.

That's why we need more white allies in this fight. I rely heavily on the white women I consider allies. Otherwise, I would spend too much time trying to educate white people, most of whom refuse to listen to me or any other Black person. White people have a much better track record of educating each other. *Why do white people have a hard time believing Black people?* Black people constantly expend energy trying to convince them we do, in fact, suffer under the weight of racism. Having white people doubt us and challenge our history is infuriating. *How can you show you're listening and actively learning about racism?* I've relayed traumatic stories of racism to white people only for them to disbelieve me or downplay my experiences. Of course, they weren't there. Yet according to them, they're better able to spot racism. *If you overheard a white person responding in this manner, how would you address it?* I can't trust anyone who tells me how I should feel or whether those feelings are valid. Any white person who thinks they know more about racism than we do can't expect us to make room for them in our lives—and certainly not in our circle of friends.

Black women have it hard enough without trying to convince white people of our experiences. That Black friend you have? Either get on board and support her or cut her loose. If you've convinced yourself that race plays no part in that friendship, you're not being much of a friend. You're causing her harm because you never bother to ask her how she's doing. *Why would you stay silent? Are you trying to avoid making mistakes that will embarrass you? Are you afraid of criticism?*

Your friend sees that you take no interest in her welfare, and your indifference hurts her. For me, I live in a state of anticipation—not of something good happening but of not knowing when the next white supremacist attack will occur. I don't know who will wield it or from what direction it will come, but it *will* come. It always does. It's just a matter of time. Unfortunately, many of those attacks come from white people I thought I knew. *How do you feel knowing Black women expect you to perpetuate racism and harm us? How would you feel if you were in a constant state of anticipation of racial violence?*

Friendships between white people and Black women can be

complicated. Although you may believe you're close friends, that relationship could be superficial because you've already shown your friend she can't trust you. **What are some ways you can build that trust?** Think about your definition of *friendship*. Perhaps you work together or meet for a yoga class. Maybe you wave to your Black neighbor as you're leaving for work. Perhaps you chat regularly over dinner or drinks, but what do you discuss? Ask yourself if your friend has ever talked about her experiences with racism. If you answered "no" because the subject never came up, there's a good chance your relationship isn't based on trust—at least not on her side. **How does discussing race/racism benefit your friendship?** I was surprised to hear many of my white allies say their parents taught them that bringing up race or even calling Black people "Black" was rude. Knowing that, I better understand why white people become defensive and angry when I talk about racism.

Back to your friend.

Racism affects our lives in such a profound way, that if your friend hasn't talked to you about it, there's definitely a reason why. **In what ways do white people fail Black women as friends?** She may not see you as a safe person with which to have that conversation. She can't trust you not to get defensive, or angry, if she discusses her experiences with you. Black people already know white people often react to stories of racism with a weaponized, not-all-white-people response that ultimately shuts down any hope of a meaningful conversation. **What are some harmful ways white people react to stories of racism? Think about how you can respond in support of a Black friend sharing her experiences with racism.**

If you're unaware of how you perpetuate racism, you won't know if she's already witnessed your racist behavior or even been on the receiving end of it. *Thinking about what you've already learned about racism, what tools can you use to help you recognize when you've harmed your friend?* She also might be avoiding the vortex white people suck many of us into—the one where you expect us to teach you about racism. You don't offer any compensation. You just drop that request like it's nothing and have the audacity to get angry when we say it's not our job to offer you a free education. If you're one of those white people who peppers your Black friends with questions about racism and you're not open to what you hear, then of course your friend doesn't trust you enough to have a frank conversation. While she may call you a friend, you're not someone with which she can discuss her experiences with racism. *Why should she waste her time trying to educate an unwilling student? How can you prepare yourself so you're open to this conversation?*

One of the worst comments a white woman can say to me is, "I don't see color." *Why is this comment unacceptable for white people to say?* I wish white people would stop saying that. It's a blatant lie. Everyone sees color. There's nothing wrong with that. By constantly saying you don't see color, you're actually admitting you refuse to acknowledge my history, culture, and experiences. You turn a blind eye to the stark differences between how society treats me and how it treats you. If you've told your friend you don't see color, you've purposely erased a part of her identity. You've given her every reason to distrust you if you can easily make the decision to ignore the sides of her you deem unimportant. *How does claiming color blind-ness hinder your progress as an ally?*

I've also encountered white people who claim their friend-ships with Black women means they can't possibly be rac-ist. Their Black friend may have even told them they're not racist. Friendships are complicated that way. When a Black woman and a white woman build a long-term friendship and go through difficult life experiences together, the Black woman may feel like she can't confront her friend the same way she would other white people. She really wants to talk to her friend about her racism. However, she knows she may lose that relationship if she does. *How would you work toward having this discussion with your Black friend?*

As an ally, you never want your friend to give you a pass. *Why is this important?* For example, if a Black person calls you out on something racist you said or did, believe them. Don't use your Black friend, spouse, or child as a shield to prevent yourself from being held accountable for your actions. That only makes us wonder how you treat these people you sup-posedly love if you can behave so abhorrently toward *us*. You're exhibiting racism, and no amount of "Well, my Black friend doesn't think I'm a racist" changes that. You're still a white person refusing to hold yourself accountable. Your friend values your relationship enough to keep you in her life. However, you must value that friendship enough to see her as a friend *and* a Black woman. *Why is it important to be held accountable when you perpetuate racism?*

You may have been surrounded by racists your whole life. Perhaps every generation of your family is filled with them, and racism is all you know. Because of that, you see Black people as one-dimensional beings who don't warrant a deeper understanding or connection. In the meantime, the friendship with your Black friend is great because—let me guess — she's not like other Black people. **How does this comment negatively affect your Black friend?** That friendship gives you satisfaction. You feel better about yourself because of that relationship. But that's not a friendship in its truest form.

Real interracial friendships explore the important subject of race. Both people understand that piece can't be overlooked. So you support your friend and strive to educate yourself about her struggles. Black people are *Black*. That means we encounter racism and white supremacy as often as white people embrace white privilege. It's every day and everywhere. If you befriend a Black person and avoid understanding the racism we endure, you're not looking for a friend. You're looking for an excuse for your own racism. You're using your friend to assuage your own guilt. You can't be her friend while also holding on to your white supremacy and racism. **What aspects of your friendship are missing if you don't talk to your Black friend about race?**

White people may feel it's unfair of us to distrust them. However, they only have themselves to blame because they refuse to see us as individuals. Instead of understanding we're all different, they categorize us either as good Black people worthy of them or bad Black people worthy of nothing. These good Black people are ones white people believe exhibit behaviors or achievements they respect. For example, as a Black woman, I've heard countless times from white people that I'm "well-spoken" or "articulate." **What are white people really saying here?** That comment is insulting enough without adding: "You're not like other Black people." They smile as they say it because they honestly believe this is a compliment. However, they're only showing me they've bought into every racial stereotype about us. We're not real people to them. They only see us as a compilation of how the media and pop culture portray us—usually as gang members, prostitutes, criminals, deadbeats, and welfare queens. **What words have you used to describe Black people? How do you think these stereotypes have affected us?**

If you've told your friend that she's the exception to the Black race, you're perpetrating racist stereotypes. You're not fooling her. She knows exactly what you're saying. You believe you're superior to people like her. You've never taken the time to even consider the possibility that your beliefs are wrong and racist. You give her no reason to ever trust you. You've shown her exactly who you are and what you believe. You believe white people embody acceptable societal characteristics and Black people don't. The ones who do are the exception and never the rule. **Do you believe certain characteristics or achievements can only be attributed to white people?**

The idea that this mix of "good" characteristics is tied to whiteness and can somehow save us from racism baffles me. White people are legitimately surprised that I have two college degrees, as if higher education isn't a goal Black women aspire to achieve. They're shocked I've never had children. That's because they see Black women as promiscuous and irresponsible. So of course, we *all* have children and by multiple men. *Why is this a dangerous stereotype for Black women?* They see Black men as menacing criminals just waiting for the opportunity to inflict violence upon them. That's why I tell white people not to believe what they see on TV or what they hear amongst their white friends. I encourage them to question everything and educate themselves about racism. *Are you surprised when you encounter Black women who don't fit the stereotypes? Why?*

White people are uncomfortable hearing about our stories of racism. They call us divisive because we speak out about issues in the Black community and confront racism and oppression head-on. Yet they've convinced themselves that, if Black people simply stopped talking about it, somehow we would all come together in a kumbaya moment and racism would miraculously end. *Why are white people reluctant to talk about race?*

White people claim we're all one race—the *human* race. Here's the problem with that. If they actually believed that, they wouldn't methodically create rules and pass policies to the contrary. If white people actually treated us as equals, we wouldn't constantly have to fight just to have our voices heard. We wouldn't be marching and protesting just so we aren't shot down in the street like animals. We would already have the right to live our lives without the invasion of white supremacy. White people who tout this one-race mantra are gaslighting us. They are very much aware of the hierarchy of color and that they reside firmly at the top. *If they really don't see color, why is it that most white people have no Black friends? How do they know to avoid including Black people in their inner circles?* White people must be honest about why they have no Black friends or, if they do have one, why they're still so clueless about racism.

I've encountered white people who have Black family members or friends yet who are incredibly racist. That's partly because the Black people in their lives refuse to call them out. *How does using Black friends and family to shield you from repercussions harm them?* These white people say they understand racism because they've experienced it firsthand. Since they've witnessed it happening to someone else, they know what it feels like. *Why is this detrimental to anti-racism work? What does this white person misunderstand about racism?* This is nonsense. Co-opting racist experiences is never a good idea. These white people believe that saying they've faced racism is helpful—that somehow it brings them closer to us—but it only proves how little they understand the history of racism and the Black experience in this country. *How would you begin working with this white person?* That's why it's important that white people educate themselves. That education truly is the foundation of being an effective ally.

This book is only the beginning of your journey. Once you delve into becoming an ally and form relationships both with other white people and Black women, you'll understand how much work there is to do. *What do you hope to gain out of these relationships? What questions do you have?* White people harm us daily. They don't even consider the consequences of what they do to us. So when you're working through this book, don't ask your Black friend any questions related to this process. Don't ask her to read your journal. Don't ask her to educate you. It's selfish to further harm her by asking her to go through this journey with you. You're not being a friend if you want her to listen to your racism. If you've already thought about asking her questions about this process, you're either trying to cut corners or you're seeking confirmation that you're one of the "good" white people. *How does asking for her help when you're addressing racism within yourself hurt her?* Even if your friend says she trusts you, that doesn't mean you've gone through life without hurting other Black people. You have. Sometimes we give our white friends a pass when we shouldn't. So don't get hung up on her stamp of approval. You can still grow and be a better friend to her. That's because allies are made, not born. Every white person has the capacity to weaponize their whiteness. That includes you. Don't make the rookie mistake of believing you're different and would never do anything to perpetuate racism. Real allies know this just isn't true. So do the work and protect your friend from your racism. That means there will be times when you need to protect her from *you*. Even after you finish this book, commit to harming less and helping more. That's what your friend would want from you. *How will you protect her during the times you're struggling as an ally?*

Another reason I tell you not to rope her into this work is that she'll probably agree to help you. *What do you lose on your ally journey by asking her to help you?* It's selfish of you to allow her to do any of your work, especially since you've probably never even talked to her about racism. You don't want this process to be the beginning of that conversation with her. Instead, tell her that you want to be an ally so you're a better friend to her. Tell her you know you've harmed her in the past, and you want to make amends by doing the work of becoming anti-racist. Thank her for her friendship. *How do these acknowledgments help you become a better ally to her and other Black women?*

White people don't understand how much damage they do to us in the name of friendship. Think about the times you've heard family, friends, or coworkers express their racism. *What racist conversations have you witnessed in your inner circle? Did you speak up? Why or why not?* If you've never considered how those words could affect your friend, you clearly aren't thinking as an ally. A true ally would confront that racism because allyship means you don't give anyone a pass. You're never silent because you know silence means you're complicit in our oppression. Allies never ignore racism, no matter who the person is or how much you love them. *Why must you confront any racism you see?* Allyship also involves having those conversations with Black friends. However, this isn't the time to ask them invasive, harmful questions. It simply means letting your friend know you're fighting racism with her and you want to be an ally *for* her. You can tell her you welcome any criticism or feedback she wants to give you. Let her decide when, or if, she wants to open up to you. Your job is to lay a foundation where she knows she can talk to you. *What are some steps you can take to lay that foundation of trust without pressuring your friend to talk to you before she's ready? How will you prevent yourself from pushing her into conversations she's not ready to have?*

REINFORCE YOUR KNOWLEDGE

Use your journal to answer the following questions and discuss how you completed the actions.

Scenario

You invite your Black friend over for dinner. It's the first time she's meeting your husband. As you sit down to eat, your husband starts talking about all the stories about racism on the news. He says, "We focus too much on race in this country. We should just treat people like people." From your friend's face, you can tell she's upset. What education can you provide to your husband in that moment to support your friend (remember that, as an ally, you confront racism everywhere)?

Question 1: For what reasons would you hesitate to talk about race with a Black friend? Why?

Question 2: What racism have you exhibited that could harm a Black friend? What are some steps you can take right now to change those behaviors?

Question 3: How would you show a Black woman that you respect and appreciate her friendship? What behaviors should you avoid?

Action

Choose three questions from this chapter related to friendships with Black women to ask yourself and three other allies. You can either work with your affinity group or with people in your racial justice group. Take note of the responses. What answers stood out to you? What surprised you?

Part IV

BECOMING A TRUE ALLY

·····································

Week 4

Chapter 10

NO ALLY THEATER

Avoiding the pitfalls of perfectionism
and performative behavior

llies are vulnerable to behaviors that hinder their progress. That's because of the temptation to cut corners and
seek praise for their efforts. Whether they're new to the work
or have done anti-racism for years, perfection and performative allyship remain two toxic traits that prevent them from
becoming dependable allies ready and willing to fight for Black
women. Although these concepts look different, they serve the
same function—to give the illusion that you're an ally, when in
reality you have no vested interest in that journey.

Perfectionism means you want every racial justice encounter in which you participate to go perfectly. You fear criticism of your efforts so much, that you refuse to take even the
smallest risks. You're terrified of making mistakes and having
anyone correct you. You stay quiet, hoping to fly under the
radar. You've convinced yourself that joining an anti-racism
group and reading materials make you an ally. You've will-
ingly chosen to remove yourself from the actual work, instead
watching from the sidelines.

Remember what I've said throughout this handbook—"ally" means "action." The theory of racism serves to educate you, but if you're doing nothing with that education, you're upholding white supremacy and protecting racism. *How does not educating yourself or others affect the racial justice movement?* No one does this work perfectly. Everyone makes mistakes, including me. When white people focus on trying to be perfect, they don't engage with other allies to learn about their own racism or how to confront it in others. Perfectionism is a white-centering behavior that puts your comfort ahead of anti-racism work (I covered the importance of discomfort in Chapter 3).

Allyship requires a commitment to continually educating yourself and others. Real allies know they must take action to create real change for Black women. *From reading this book and writing in your journal, what goals do you immediately want to accomplish as a new ally?* The actions you perform further your understanding of racism both within yourself and to help guide others. If you never put yourself out there and risk making a mistake, your silence lends itself to the very issues we're fighting. *How does white supremacy grow from your silence?* I've heard several excuses why white people don't speak up: *They're afraid to say anything. They don't want to make a mistake. They don't know what to say. They're scared of being called out. They're listening, and that's how they learn best.*

Let's look more closely at the excuses white people use to avoid doing real ally work.

If you're afraid to speak up, how do you think you're fighting racism? *Why do white people claim reading about racism actually fights it?* I keep repeating that just reading isn't enough.

You must act. Think about why you're afraid. Are you shy or an introvert? I'm also an introvert. Many white allies I work with are by nature introspective people. Yet they regularly speak up and confront racism. I doubt it's easy for them, but they know that's their job as an ally. *How does discomfort benefit your progress as an ally?* These allies know that staying silent means they're part of the systemic racism that keeps Black women oppressed.

Making mistakes is part of being human. Whether you're learning how to become an ally or learning how to use the Internet, you'll falter. Find your lessons in those missteps so you can do better next time. *Why must allies make mistakes and learn from them?* I use the Internet comparison because I've taught many people how to surf the Web. Most of the time, these individuals haven't had access to computers and aren't comfortable using them. I'll give you the same advice I give them: Practice. That's how you master any skill. *Why are scenarios and role-playing important in ally work?* You won't break the Internet when you make a mistake. *You* also won't break if you make a mistake. Perhaps you're afraid of embarrassment, which goes right back to discomfort. Remember that feeling uncomfortable leads to growth. Whatever situation in your ally journey frightens you or forces you out of your comfort zone guides you to a new lesson that you can teach other white people. *How do these lessons help you influence other white people?*

If you encounter any white allies who claim to never make mistakes in this work, explain to them why perfectionism is detrimental to anti-racism work. *How will you begin a conversation about perfectionism?* Suggest this handbook and provide them with the same education I'm giving you here. It's a dangerous narrative to claim you've never made a mistake doing anti-racism work. Of course you have. It's interesting that perfectionism comes up at all. We forget that the things in which we've gained proficiency, we've mastered through practicing, making mistakes, and learning from them. How do you learn a new subject in school or a new skill at work? *What happens to your growth as an ally if you refuse to make mistakes?* It's all about practicing until you understand this new concept or ability. Keep that in mind when you make excuses about why you don't speak up. The white allies I trust readily admit they've screwed up numerous times and that they continue to make mistakes. *When educating other white people, why should you admit you've made mistakes?* They use those stories to educate other white people. They never push a perfectionist narrative because they know that is counterintuitive to becoming an effective ally.

White people also will witness blatant racism in silence because they don't know what to say. *What responses have you learned so far that will help you when you witness racism?* At this point, you've learned numerous resources to use in these situations. You should have role-played various scenarios so you're more comfortable having these conversations. If you're still struggling about what to say in most of these situations, you haven't yet internalized these lessons. Figure out how to propel yourself into action. Ask other white people how they began having difficult conversations with other white people. You'll learn that allies are spurred to action for various reasons. Maybe a specific encounter turned into a catalyst for them to change and speak up. *In what situations would you speak up about racism? How could you help other white people who are hesitant to confront racism?* Perhaps they've decided that finding their voice is more important than staying comfortable. Consider the reasons why you want to do this work and start educating other people you see struggling to begin their own journey. You may never be comfortable speaking up, but discovering your own voice puts Black women that much closer to achieving equality. Remember that every lesson you learn can and should be shared with other white people working to become allies.

When white people are afraid of being called out, what they're saying is their fear is more important than actually acknowledging they made a mistake and harmed one of us. *What tips would you give them to overcome that fear?* Call-outs/call-ins are never fun, and you shouldn't expect them always to be this educational exchange of information. Black women have a right to express anger and dismay at you because of your racism. *What can you do to prevent yourself from getting defensive in these situations?* There's a lesson in that, too. Your words or actions have caused us pain. You must learn from that mistake, and that means another person should confront you on it. If I call you out, I'll tell you how your actions affected me. Part of the reason you're afraid is because my angry reaction makes you uncomfortable.

It all comes back to your wanting to avoid anything that creates discomfort for you. It's another behavior that centers your feelings over my oppression. That's not the mindset of allies. It won't kill you to listen to our anger. If you're called out by another white person, listen just as closely as you would to a Black woman speaking. Call-outs should help you understand what you did wrong. Whether the recipient speaks angrily shouldn't diminish the importance of the message. **Why is this important to remember?** Take in those words and process them. Learn how to do better the next time. Remember that, as an ally, you also should call in other white people. Your own experiences will help you navigate those conversations. **What is one tool you've learned that will help you teach others?**

I've encountered many white people who have read every book about racism and watched every documentary. Yet they don't say a word when they're actually faced with a racist person. Their internal dialogue tells them that somehow reading and listening make them at least better than white people who haven't even done that. **Why would white people compare themselves in this way?** The problem is they've only used those resources to convince us they're doing the work when, in fact, they're simply going through the motions. They haven't made any effort to address their own racism. Until they do that internal work, they're useless to Black women as an ally. Allyship doesn't mean assigning yourself homework and stopping once you've completed it. If you haven't even considered how to use that information to work on your own personal growth or teach others, you've wasted your time even picking it up. **Why must you use the information you learn? How does that help you as an ally?** That's like reading every medical textbook on surgery and thinking you're now qualified to operate. It doesn't work that way.

Think about ally work as your residency. It's where you're applying the techniques you've learned. It's how you practice precisely excising racism. The more you do the work, the more exact you become in learning how to use the knowledge you've gained. Don't let that education go to waste. Do something with it. If you're unsure how to start, ask your accountability partner or the allies in your racial justice group. *What questions would you ask them to help you take action?* By now you should be comfortable seeking out other white people to ask them how they overcame challenges you're facing. This should be no different. If you're afraid to speak up, seek out other allies for advice. It's easy to fall into the trap of simply reading and listening. However, you must both take in that information, and disseminate it. One doesn't work without the other.

Once you begin talking to other white people about racism, you'll quickly realize how difficult it is to change anyone else's mind. You'll get frustrated and angry at the number of racists you encounter who are happy to remain that way. *How will you keep yourself motivated to continue?* However, you'll achieve victories, too. Once you've gotten someone to listen and think about their own racism, you'll feel like you've accomplished your goal. You should be proud of that achievement. Enjoy it, but never forget the reason you're educating others. You're fighting racism, and in that way, you're also fighting for Black women. *Why should you remember the ultimate goal of ally work?*

Black women are watching you fight for us. We know who takes this work seriously and who wants accolades while they pretend to be an ally. There will always be white people who know the right words to say so they receive accolades—or cookies—from Black women. They want us to compliment them and tell them what a great job they're doing. These people started out on the right path, but they detoured as soon as our praise became more important than continuing their journey to become a real ally. *How does seeking praise hurt your progress as an ally? How does that behavior affect racial justice work?* These performative allies are always ready for a show. They jump onstage to do their ally "skit" anytime they think one of us is watching.

Years ago, I encountered one of the worst performative allies I've ever met. This white woman—whom I'll call Jean—put on Academy Award-worthy productions with her long, rambling lectures to other white women she deemed unworthy of being called "allies." *What do you immediately see as a problem with Jean?* I became aware of her when she joined "Real Talk." At first I was impressed by what I thought was her passion and dedication to racial justice work. I saw her educating other white people. However, I later learned from other allies that her idea of educating solely involved arguments and insults. Instead of working with other white women, she chose to humiliate them.

"Real Talk" is a space where white women can learn to become allies. We've come across many white women who have flown their racist white woman flag and refused any education or accountability. *Why do you think they're unwilling to be held responsible for their harm? How would you try to help them?* Most of the time those conversations turn confrontational. Usually the woman "flounces" from the group. "Flouncing" happens when a white woman writes a long, dramatic post about how the group did her wrong before leaving. She takes no responsibility for her behavior.

However, the white women who sincerely want to learn

from their mistakes and do better? They ask for that education. They try to listen to criticism of their behavior and learn from it. In "Real Talk," another white woman works with them so they understand what they did. They work in a separate space we call "The Mending Room." That requires a certain amount of patience, but more importantly, it takes self-reflection on the part of the person doing the educating. *What happens if the person educating hasn't done the internal work to understand their own racism?* A white person working with someone who has screwed up must draw from her own experiences to successfully help the other person understand where they went wrong. Otherwise, it's a hollow learning experience for the one asking for help. The conversation won't ring true. That's what happened with Jean.

I began hearing that Jean's idea of a "mending" was to viciously confront every white woman and go on the attack. She wanted to be known as the white woman who went in the hardest on other white women. *Why is this a barrier to actually educating anyone?* She put aside any semblance of education. It was all about treating the other person like trash. It happened almost every single time, no matter who she called in for a mending. I also noticed that, when Jean was called in to address her own racism, she refused to do the work. She became combative and stubborn. She even told another white woman that only Black women could educate her. She added that she had nothing to learn from white women. *What is the problem with Jean asking Black women to educate her?*

Jean eventually left the group, but I would see her on friends' Facebook pages calling out other white women. She had gotten even worse. She used the same tactics, but it was obvious she loved the attention she received from Black women who were grateful that any white woman spoke out for them. I saw them praising her. While I did warn some Black women about her performative motives, most kept her around, probably because she was one of the few white women they knew who was willing to confront other white people. **How will you encourage other white people to speak up and confront racism?**

Jean enjoyed the power she possessed. She became a go-to "ally" to address "educating" other white people. I saw her regularly tearing them apart, even when that person obviously wanted to learn from her mistake. **Why would Jean choose not to actually educate other white women?** She didn't see a reason to educate anyone if she received praise for coming in like a bull in a china shop. Jean was smart enough to hide the fact that she wouldn't address her own racism and white supremacy. From the outside, all you saw was a white woman fiercely protecting Black women from harm—except that was the furthest from the truth. Remember she said she only wanted Black women to educate her? Requiring us to teach her was bad enough. However, after a Black woman actually tried to help her when she misstepped, Jean rejected that woman and her wisdom with all the white tears and fragility she claimed to loathe in other white women. **Why did Jean refuse to be educated by a Black woman even though she stated we were the only ones capable of teaching her?**

Performative allyship is common in racial justice work. However, if you regularly check in with yourself and your accountability partner to discuss conversations you've had about race and take an honest assessment of the motivations behind those conversations, you'll recognize when you've shifted from anti-racist to performative ally. *What other reasons would you check in with yourself when doing ally work?* If your main concern is whether Black women praise you, you're not educating yourself or anyone else. You're centering your feelings of self-worth around getting our attention for work you're not even doing. You're lying to us, and you're lying to yourself. You can leave ally theater when you refocus your efforts on the fight, not yourself. *Why is centering yourself counterproductive to your work as an ally?*

Performative allyship is dangerous to Black women. White people who want to impress us with their antics are the same ones willing to sabotage us and our work if we don't applaud them for their performance. They're the ones who collect Black women by joining different groups and pulling the same ally stunts in each one. They see us as shiny objects they can manipulate by putting us on pedestals. They don't see us as Black women fighting for our humanity. That's not allyship in any of its forms. It's performative, and it's racist. Unfortunately, white people who indulge in ally theater are common in racial justice circles. *Why are performative allies so common? How do they harm the movement?* Look around any racial justice space, and you'll find these people. Oftentimes, they insinuate themselves into the confidences of someone they believe has power within that group. They lie their way into spaces with Black women so they can figure out the inner workings and, if necessary, try to pit Black women against each other. They're not above creating discourse amongst us so they can lend a sympathetic ear, if needed.

Performative allies are the very ones focused on a mythical hierarchy that most Black women don't recognize or validate. Allies who rank their allyship against other white people and consistently place themselves at the top have no interest in racial justice work. ***What is the danger of ranking allies?*** To them, the ally arena is one big stage and Black women are the unwitting audience members. Jean was one such ally. She even created a "Dangerous White Women" list and passed it around to the Black women she knew. I heard about it when some white women in "Real Talk" told me they were included on it. ***Why would Jean create this list? Why does this harm anti-racism work?*** Of course, Jean decided *she* was the expert on who was worthy of being called an ally, even though she should never bestow that title on herself or any other white person. That didn't stop her, however. She waded into toxic white woman territory but said she was protecting Black women from any white women who would harm them. Most of the Black women she manipulated had no idea that Jean refused to do any real ally work. ***Why is it important that Black women see you working on your own racism?*** I watched as she denigrated white women whom I considered some of the best racial justice allies I knew. However, they were also ones who tried to educate her when she made mistakes—and she made plenty of them. Because of that, she added them to her list. Most of those women lost touch with Black women they highly respected. Jean used her influence to turn Black women against allies who were actually showing up for us. It was sickening to watch.

I want to be clear that none of these Black women are gullible. That's not what's at play here. When we have so few white allies who are willing to stand up for us, we depend on them to confront racism in other white people. Because that's the only side of Jean they ever saw, these women didn't know that she collected us like trophies. **What harmful traits does Jean possess that make her a performative ally?** They didn't know she used Black women to fulfill her own yearning to belong and feel needed. In essence, she took advantage of us to make herself feel better. It's no different than the allies I mentioned previously who believed racial justice work should make them feel good, and it was up to Black people to make that happen.

We also see performative allyship at play related to the Black Lives Matter movement. White people now use #BLM as a cool hashtag to add to their social media profiles and not much else. **How is this performative?** I've encountered numerous white people on Twitter with that hashtag who have no knowledge of what the movement even means. Their commitment to "allyship" begins and ends with that hashtag. In 2020, the music industry started a movement called #BlackoutTuesday. You may not remember the name, but you probably remember people replacing the images on their social media with a black square. Maybe you did it, too? Created by two Black women, the goal was to bring awareness to racial inequality. Sounds great, right?

However, once #BlackoutTuesday started, it drowned out the very issue it wanted to highlight. Because people hashtagged #BlackLivesMatter along with #BlackoutTuesday, when you searched for information on BLM, your results included a bunch of pages with black square profiles instead of taking you to pages that were actually about BLM. *Why do you think #BlackoutTuesday was so popular on social media but it didn't create any real change?* I didn't participate. Many of us on social media didn't see the point. I refused to replace my image with a black square. Black people are silenced enough in this country. I wasn't participating in any movement asking me to censor myself. White people ate this up, however. They thought they were *doing* something. *What could white people have done after #BlackoutTuesday?* Just like posting #BlackLivesMatter on their social media pages, white people were giving the illusion of supporting us while going about their white privileged lives in the same ways they always had. They continued to ignore the real-life problems Black people faced because of racism. They didn't speak up, and they didn't show up. They convinced themselves that these shows of support were enough. They didn't need to actually confront racism. *How are white privilege and the refusal to show up related?* They must have been relieved to discover how easy it was to be an ally to Black people. While I love social media, too many white people have fallen into these performative acts that only dilute the anti-racism message.

From my own online experiences with these white people, many are just as racist as anyone on the right. *Why would white liberals also embrace white supremacy?* They're not educating themselves, and they're not interested in educating anyone else. No, that's untrue. They're quite interested in educating *me* and other Black people about racism. That's after they've listened to some podcasts and read a few articles. Now they want to impart that knowledge on the very people those resources are discussing and who, through firsthand experience, are experts on the subject. Performative allyship is toxic in this way. These white people don't understand how they uphold racism and white supremacy. **How do they do this?** They're too busy taking advantage of situations where they can stand in the spotlight. These are the very people who speak over us and for us, all in the name of allyship.

After the murder of George Floyd, many corporations posted #BlackLivesMatter on their social media pages and subsequently joined the ranks of performative allyship. That's because most organizations are anything but diverse at the executive levels. They're lily white and almost exclusively men. We have to look more broadly than #BlackLivesMatter and its relationship to police brutality. We must examine economic inequality, too. If a corporation were serious about racial justice, wouldn't they work on diversifying their organization at every level? Countless times, I've seen photos of diversity committees made up exclusively of white men. No women or minorities were included. Obviously they're not interested in real change if the people they claim to support aren't even given a voice in these discussions. Many corporations employ Diversity, Equity, and Inclusion (DEI) officers whose job should be to address issues within the company. These positions increased when racial justice became a regular topic of discussion. Oftentimes, DEI officers help address diversity issues within the organization, such as culture and diversity hiring. From my own experience, that simply meant that I had to assimilate into a corporate environment with no interest in changing its toxic environment to accommodate me.

DEI initiatives are a mixed bag, and too many of these positions are created to make it seem as if organizations care about every employee—including the ones they deem different from their norm. Personally, if your organization is mostly white, that's by design. Your hiring practices and retention efforts aren't prioritizing diversity. Your DEI efforts are performative at best. Organizations who want to diversify their workforce will do just that. I refuse to believe for a second that these places can't find qualified people from diverse backgrounds. They are deliberately, systemically keeping those companies controlled by white men and employed with a majority of white people.

Perfectionism probably contributes to the performative allyship of organizations. While executives and human resources are willing to research and take a chance on initiatives such as organizational changes that potentially affect every one of their employees, they won't lend the same energy toward understanding the value of diversifying their companies. I've worked in such places, and I felt both invisible and hypervisible there. My contributions were not wanted, and the dearth of Black employees told me that the unique perspective of people like me wasn't valued. The irony is that studies show, when organizations diversity, they increase their bottom line. Their profits grow, which makes sense. A diversified organization means a diversity of experiences to bring to the table. The idea that it's too risky to hire more non-white people means that their comfort in coming to work and seeing mostly people who look like them is more important than the company's success. Remember I said discomfort gives way to growth.

Organizations constantly make decisions they hope will benefit their company. Unfortunately, most don't seem to care that prioritizing whiteness in their ranks means never achieving the level of success possible with a diversified workforce, especially at the ranks where vital decisions are made. *Why do you think companies claim to support diversity but don't follow through?* The common thread is white people saying all the right things, then simply not showing up for Black women. The participants in the study on activism burnout that I mentioned in Chapter 8 are a prime example of what happens when performative allies do nothing to actually fight racism. Like those activists, Black women burn out juggling their daily lives and fighting for equality, oftentimes with little support from white people. *How would anti-racism work benefit from more white allies?* While these performative allies prance around throwing out quotes and lecturing other white people, we're left to do the real labor. Performative allies selfishly take credit for work they haven't even started, let alone finished. Jean will happily tell you how she shaped the training in "Real Talk." Yet again, she will center herself by inflating her importance in educating others. In actuality, she manipulated ally training to her advantage by not participating in her own education and eagerly shouting down other white women who made mistakes. *Why is Jean dangerous to anti-racism work and to Black women?* Her influence on our training is merely as a cautionary tale to other white women not to follow in her footsteps and for Black women not to be fooled into believing that the loudest white person in the crowd is always someone we should call an ally.

REINFORCE YOUR KNOWLEDGE

Use your journal to answer the following questions and discuss how you completed the actions.

Scenario

You notice a white woman in your racial justice group aggressively calling out another white person. She's not educating him. She doesn't provide resources. You've seen her do this numerous times. As usual, she doesn't work with the other white person so that he can understand and acknowledge his harm. She doesn't try to help him learn from his mistakes. She simply criticizes his behavior and belittles him. What would you say to her? What would you say to the white man? What resources can you use in this situation?

Question 1: Why do you think white people become performative allies? If you saw yourself becoming performative, how would you get back on track?

Question 2: How can perfectionism prevent you from learning about yourself as an ally?

Action

Meet with your accountability partner or affinity group and discuss ways you can avoid perfectionism and performative allyship. Brainstorm how you spot these traits and what to do if you start exhibiting these behaviors. Talk about how you'll hold each other accountable. Each person must agree to listen if any other member calls them out. Discuss how to help each other work with someone they see doing ally theater. How will you educate them? What resources can you use?

Chapter 11

STRATEGICALLY SILENT

Amplifying Black female voices and passing the mic

You should now be regularly seeking information to continuously educate yourself and other white people. Part of that education includes amplifying our voices, and you've already been doing that through your discussions about racism. You've also joined racial justice groups to listen and learn from Black women. You're learning from your own mistakes and passing on that knowledge to other potential allies. **What resources have you found most effective to amplify our voices?** You're reading books by and about Black people. You're watching documentaries to learn about our history, culture, and experiences. You're continuously building your library of resources so you're an effective educator. Within those spaces whose missions focus on racial justice, you're learning the importance of decentering yourself when you're listening to our experiences with racism and how white people contribute to its growth. You're always looking for ways to show others how they can help with this fight. **What challenges have you encountered in teaching others?** You're bearing witness in these spaces that prioritize our needs, something that rarely happens in the real world. You see us as people fighting for equality and our very existence. You're taking those lessons and making sure they don't evaporate within those groups. As you grow into a better ally, you try to guide others toward beginning their own journeys.

Amplifying our voices and passing the mic go hand in hand. I want you to look around for ways to pass the mic so that Black women can be heard. *Other than Black women, who else benefits when our voices are heard?* There are plenty of opportunities to help us. As an ally, you must seek out situations and learn to speak up anytime you see our voices being diminished by other white people. *How will you begin learning how to recognize these situations?* White people regularly attempt to silence us. I've personally experienced this silencing more times than I can count. Several years ago, I attended a meeting to discuss new technologies the company might want to introduce to the public. A white woman led the meeting. She asked attendees their opinions about technologies we had seen demonstrated at recent conferences. After her first question, several of us raised our hands. She pointed to someone and listened to their answer. For one hour, she asked questions and pointed to people to answer or give their opinions. I raised my hand every time. The last time I raised it, I was the only person with my hand up. She glanced at me and said, "Okay, let's move on to another topic." I put my hand down.

Was I overreacting? Did I misunderstand? I might have convinced myself that this racist microaggression was simply an oversight. However, after the meeting, some of my coworkers expressed their disbelief at the way she treated me. I barely knew the woman leading the meeting, so it wasn't as if we had a history of conflict. I was the only Black person in that meeting. I understood that she didn't want or need my opinion and was letting me know in the most humiliating way—in front of my fellow coworkers, many of whom I considered friends. *Why do you think nobody spoke up?* I was angry—both at her and the white people who said nothing during the meeting. This is called a "microaggression." While her behavior wasn't overtly racist, targeting the only Black person in attendance was a clear indication she didn't want me there. But this was also a chance for a white person to pass me the mic. It would have taken one white person to stand up and say, "Lecia raised her hand several times and wasn't invited to give input. Her opinion also has value." That's passing the mic. This woman wasn't willing to listen to me, and anyone witnessing her behavior could have asked why she chose to ignore me. They could have held her accountable and ensured I had the same opportunity as they did to participate in that space. Instead she ignored me while they silently looked on. *What would you have done if you witnessed what happened to me? How would you pass the mic?*

Passing the mic sometimes means a physical mic, such as centering our voices during protests and marches. As an ally, you should participate in these events, but always be aware when you're silencing our voices in favor of your own. Passing the mic also requires that you pay attention to situations where Black women are overlooked and marginalized. Your voice probably will be the lone one speaking up, but that's what we need from allies. *How will you prepare yourself to speak up?* We want our opinions valued on the same level as white people. Black women shouldn't have to fight this hard for the little bit of space we're given in these white-centered environments. Allies calling out white people who are unwilling to pass us the mic can change that dynamic. When allies protest efforts to silence us, they create the expectation that Black women who want to be heard are given that opportunity. If white people still refuse to give us a voice, they should expect allies to speak up and demand that they do. *What does this teach a white person who refuses to pass the mic?* When you demand that we're passed the mic, you're creating real change and bringing us closer to racial equality.

I want you to think about ways you can amplify our voices that have immediate results. Let's discuss how you can uplift us and directly address racial inequality and systemic racism. *Why should you strive to support us in ways that immediately create change? Why should you speak up in the moment?* While marching and voting are important tools, one of the most effective ways you can support us is to question the status quo and ask why Black women aren't represented in a space. Challenging other white people using the information in this chapter helps pass the mic and amplify our voices because you'll question hiring practices and wonder aloud why you don't see us in your organizations. You'll demand to know why our voices aren't present and explain why those voices are necessary. You'll begin supporting our leadership and business ventures. You can pass the mic to Black women by pushing for us to have a seat at the table and ensuring our voices are heard once we get there. *How can you provide space for Black women in your organizations and in other places?*

In 2020, the #SharetheMicNow campaign saw Black women take over Instagram accounts of famous white women. The campaign took off and was repeated across the country. I mention this specific campaign for a reason: It's still alive and well. *The Washington Post* delved into the promises made by top corporations such as Apple, Johnson & Johnson, Procter & Gamble since May 2020 (the month of George Floyd's murder) to commit a collective $49.5 billion to racial justice. The newspaper discovered how the monies were spent and reported its findings in August 2021. Ninety percent of those funds was allocated to investments and mortgages, both of which equated to profits for those corporations. Banking giants JPMorgan Chase and Bank of America received the bulk of that business. About $70 million of the money was earmarked for criminal justice reform.[18] When we look at the amount of money given to already successful banks, we must ask this question: Why didn't these corporations consider channeling enough funds into Black-owned banks so they could better serve their communities' Black homeowners and business owners?

18   Jan, T., McGregor, J. & Hoyer, M. (2021, August 23). Corporate America's $50 billion promise. *The Washington Post.* https://www. washingtonpost.com/business/interactive/2021/george-floyd-corporate-america-racial-justice/

These organizations seem to believe that simply spending money will solve the problem. They didn't consider how to allocate those funds in way that directly addressed economic inequalities. However, economic inequity is only one challenge Black people face. We must be willing to address the systemic racism that allows these economic divides to persist between Black and white people.

More Black women are getting the chance to share their thoughts and tell their stories. Every racial justice campaign needs clear goals and a way to achieve them. **Why does it help to have stated goals?** If you attended any Women's March, did you seek ways to keep the momentum going? Not every march, protest, or campaign will give you instructions for next steps you can do. In those cases, do your own research and come up with ways to continue racial justice work after the march is over. Find ways to support Black women that make real substantive changes in our lives. That could include supporting businesses, political campaigns, community activism, or anything else where Black women are making a difference. **How could you support us right now? How would you start?**

Black women have been at the forefront of racial justice work for decades. As we continue fighting for equality, we're still underrepresented in many spaces that make decisions about our lives without providing opportunities for our opinions. Black women seek representation so that we have a voice in the very policies and laws that affect us and our ability to achieve financial security. **How would this country benefit from Black women having more of a voice?** According to the Economic Policy Institute, during the COVID-19 pandemic, Black women working in essential positions were paid 11–27% less than white men. *How do you think this pay gap affects us?* Those jobs included doctors, nurses, waitresses, health care aids, and teachers. It's easy to believe the gender pay gap is based on situations such as women leaving the workforce to take care of children. However, Black women receive less pay regardless of our personal situations.

Since the time enslaved Africans were brought here, the United States has actively found ways to oppress Black people. Systemic racism doesn't just affect individuals. It affects the entire Black community. *What are some ramifications of systemic racism on Black women and the Black community?* Black women have borne the brunt of this even as our numbers continue to grow both in higher education and in the workforce. According to the Institute for Women's Policy Research, Black women make 62 cents for every dollar white men make. If more white people spoke up about these inequalities, Black women would be in better economic positions. We're earning college degrees only to enter careers where white people decide that, based on our skin color, we deserve less compensation. That decision reverberates throughout our entire lives. This pay gap affects whether we can afford health care, childcare, higher education, housing, etc. *What do you think contributes to the pay gap?*

Dr. Michelle Holder, economist and Assistant Professor of Economics at John Jay College of Criminal Justice, studied the gender wage and racial wage gaps—which she calls the "double gap"—Black women face in the workforce. *How do you think this double gap affects Black women's ability to achieve financial stability?* Even though Black women have the highest labor force participation, we are still vastly underpaid compared to white men. Dr. Holder explains how Black women provided unpaid labor as enslaved people, suffering sexual violence and loss of autonomy over their bodies. After emancipation, both Black men and Black women worked as sharecroppers, which provided them with little financial security. *What do you know about sharecropping?* After the "Great Migration," Black women worked as farm laborers and domestic workers in white households. Neither of these jobs qualified them under the New Deal to receive Social Security.

Black women have a long, well-documented history of participation in the workforce. However, corporate America benefits when it reinforces a wage gap that continues to pay us considerably less than white men. *How do companies benefit from underpaying Black women?* Dr. Holder focused on measuring how much money Black women lost because of this double gap. Throughout the study, she used highly educated Black women and compared them to white men with the same educational attainment. Using three methodologies and looking at only the private, for-profit sector, she concluded that Black women involuntarily forfeited $50 billion in wages, a considerable cost savings to the private sector. Dr. Holder concludes that, because Black women are largely undercompensated, that loss of money means they have less chance to build assets—including savings and home purchasing.[19] *How would this affect our families and future generations?*

When allies amplify our voices, you help us fight racism by ensuring our stories and experiences are heard. You're part of every organization and oftentimes make up the committees and groups responsible for deciding who to hire, who to promote, what vendors to use, etc. You must use your white privilege in these spaces to create diversity and equality. *What prevents white people from speaking up? How can you help change that?*

Human resources is one of those places where having a diversified staff goes a long way toward hiring more Black women. Black female human resources specialists can also make Black women more comfortable coming to them with questions or concerns. This is paramount because we experience workplace harassment at higher numbers than white women. I've also heard countless stories of Black women passed over for positions they're more than capable of doing in favor of less qualified white people. *How can white people help Black women get recognized and promoted?* While we toil away doing the same duties with little recognition and no chance of promotion, we're expected to be grateful we have a job. That also means we're expected to accept that organization's subservient treatment. No matter how hard we try, we're stuck. It doesn't matter how many continuing

---

19   Holder, M. (2020). *The "double-gap" and the bottom line: African American women's wage gap and corporate profits.* Roosevelt Institute. https://rooseveltinstitute.org/wp-content/uploads/2020/07/RI_DoubleGap_Report_202003.pdf

education courses, certifications, or responsibilities we take on, we'll stay in the same position at the same pay. We'll complete our duties at an exemplary level, and still white management won't acknowledge our accomplishments. They'll even bring in a white person who's less qualified than us and ask us to train them for the promotion we didn't receive. **Why do white people choose to overlook Black women's work achievements?**

White allies must recognize these situations and speak up. Don't expect us to tell you what we're experiencing. That takes a level of trust we don't have with you. How can we believe you won't run to management and risk our livelihood? Too many of you like to play double agent. You listen to us, then go tell our superiors what we said to you in confidence. As an ally, it's your job to bear witness without a word from us. **Why is this important?** Then you can act on it—especially if you know you have the ear of upper management or, better yet, you *are* upper management. It's easy to look around the room and see that we're not represented in your organization. Ask them why. If management tells you they can't find qualified Black women, ask where they've searched. Challenge them when you see one of us constantly overlooked for recognition or a promotion. Hold them accountable for why we're not working alongside you or given the same opportunities to succeed.

Black women are looking for those jobs where we can thrive. However, most of us don't have the connections that allow us a foot in door to even land the job. If we're fortunate to be hired, we aren't invited into those inner circles that lead to promotions and higher salaries. *How can white people create paths for Black women into these spaces?* I remember sitting in an all-staff meeting at my first (and only) corporate job as one of the executives talked about the numerous opportunities at that organization. However, this is the same company I previously mentioned, where I was harassed, reported it, and was consequently blackballed. I stayed in my position for almost eight years until I earned a graduate degree and switched careers. The white man who harassed me also sexually harassed a white female friend of mine. *What does that say about the white people who didn't speak up?* People knew, and no one said anything. She and I, along with another woman, reported the man to human resources. Nothing happened to him. I eventually left. Years later, he was laid off from the company, but they were unwilling to fire him for his continued harassment.

I learned some hard lessons during that time. I learned not to depend on human resources to do the right thing or my white coworkers to speak up to defend me. For eight years, they watched as I struggled with anger and depression. I fought alone as they looked on, probably thankful they weren't in my situation. *How would you have helped these white people to act?* That's why it's important that allies speak up. The white people in this organization could have amplified my voice by confirming my experiences and demanding change. *What are some ways my white coworkers could have helped me?*

Like many people, Black women aspire to own our own businesses. However, the number of Black business owners lags far behind white business owners. This affects the racial wealth gap because it limits the assets Black people can accumulate. In turn, that affects our ability to pass down generational wealth at the same levels as white people. *How does passing down wealth to the next generation help us fight racial inequality?* A 2017 study looked at how business ownership affects the racial gap. Researchers found that one reason Black business owners had lower levels of business wealth was because they were starting fewer businesses, and the ones they did start were smaller than white-owned businesses. Black-owned businesses also had smaller revenue and smaller average payrolls. Oftentimes these businesses had no other employees other than the owner of the business. In 2012, 23.9% of businesses owned by white men hired employees, compared to only 6% of Black-owned businesses. *What are the downsides of being the only employee for your business?*

The study then explored the reasons why Black-owned businesses were smaller. Because they had less personal wealth, these business owners struggled to access the needed capital to open and support their endeavors. They also had fewer assets to use when inquiring about outside capital. *How can allies in lending institutions help Black business owners?* These business owners depended more on their own money instead of seeking bank loans. In fact, many didn't even apply for bank loans, assuming their requests would be denied. Seventy-percent of Black business owners used their personal savings, compared to 64.5% of white business owners. *What are the risks of using your personal savings to start a business?* Black owners also depended on credit cards to finance their business, with 17.6% of them going this route, compared to 10.3% of white business owners. Credit scores also hindered Black business owners' ability to access capital from banks and other lending institutions. In addition, these owners faced discrimination when they applied for loans. A 2014 study used Black, Latino, and white applicants with similar characteristics. They found the Black and Latino applicants were more likely to need additional paperwork such as tax returns and personal financial assets. Loan officers were less likely to help them complete paperwork or offer their business card during the meeting. *Why do you think this discrimination still exists?*

White business owners also brought more human capital in the form of longer work histories. They had greater knowledge and experience about running businesses. In fact, almost 50% of white business owners were fifty-five or older, compared to 41% of Black business owners. Many white business owners already had connections and networks in place to help them succeed. A higher number of them had previous experience as business owners or working for themselves, which helped them successfully start and run new businesses. *How is systemic racism related to white business owners having more experience starting businesses?*

In 2014, 32.8 percent of white business owners had previous experience, compared to 28.4% of Black business owners. Compared to 23.3% of white owners, only 12.6% of Black owners had previous experience working in a family business or working for themselves. Almost twice as many white owners inherited their businesses, compared to Black and Latino owners. The age of the business and how the recipient acquired it both impact business success. In 2014, only 12.5% of Black-owned businesses were over thirty years old, compared to over 25% of white-owned businesses. One of the factors at play here was that white business owners were more likely to have inherited or been gifted an already-established business. **Why is this an advantage for white business owners?** In 2014, 70% of white owners started their business from scratch, compared to 81% of Black business owners.[20]

Despite these challenges, many Black women have fore-gone traditional workplaces in favor of starting their own businesses. Allies can help us by both supporting these endeavors and encouraging others to do the same. **How does this help us in the racial justice fight?** Amazon and Etsy now allow you to easily find businesses owned by Black women. These entrepreneurs run any type of industry and service you need. **How would you start supporting these businesses?** You're already using these services. Seek out Black women so you can directly help them succeed. Use your network to publicize it. Talk about these companies with friends and family. Post information for your Facebook and Twitter followers. Most businesses nowadays have an Internet presence. Commit to using businesses owned by Black women.

---

20   Klein, J. A. (2017, January). *Bridging the divide: How business ownership can help close the racial wealth gap.* Field at the Aspen Institute. https://www.aspeninstitute.org/wp-content/uploads/2017/01/Bridging-the-Divide.pdf

What types of businesses do you currently use that you could replace with ones owned by a Black woman? Many allies post information about the owners, the products, and what they've purchased for themselves. Supporting these businesses directly helps Black women. This is putting your money where your mouth is. Speaking up for us and supporting our businesses mean you're actively fighting for our equality. *How would you encourage other white people to support our businesses?* However, don't misunderstand my requests as a way to treat Black women as if we're not fully functioning human beings. We don't want your pity. We want—and deserve—your respect. We demand equality, and we need allies to help us achieve it. Black women also seek the American dream. Many want to start businesses to create a better life for themselves and their families. They want the means to pass down wealth to their children. Do some research and speak to other allies about how they support these Black women.

Another way you can amplify our voices is to support Black women when they run for public office. Black women are seeking office in record numbers. Look for ways to support them. Follow discussions online and in your racial justice group. *What would you hope to learn from supporting Black female candidates?* Look around your own community to find these women and volunteer to work on their campaigns. You can phone bank or knock on doors. Think about who in your own network can help you amplify her voice. Black female politicians are now getting more media exposure. It might seem like we're well-represented in politics. However, compared to our population in the United States, we're still *under*represented in public offices. There is a push to elect more Black women to office, and white allies must be ready and willing to help make this happen. **How will you find Black women to support?** During the 2020 election, we saw the power of Black women to drive change and face down racism. We've proven ourselves and what we're capable of achieving both nationally and at the grassroots level. We've organized, protested, and turned out to vote. This country has elected Kamala Harris as its first Black-South Asian female vice president. We can't stop there. **Why do white people also benefit with more Black women in office?** The year 2020 taught us that we must think both locally and nationally. Look at websites such as "Black Women in Politics" or simply google "BLACK WOMEN RUNNING FOR OFFICE" to research who's campaigning and where they're located. Research their platforms and how their beliefs align with racial justice and equality. Speak with other allies to find out who they're supporting and why they chose those candidates. **How do you benefit from asking other allies about Black women to support?**

This is also a good time to find Black female commentators discussing politics. **What would you hope to learn from Black female political commentators?** Not only will you gain a different viewpoint about current events, you'll gain insight into Black female candidates. Consider following these Black women to help with your education: White House Correspondent April Ryan, White House Deputy Press Secretary Karine Jean-Pierre, MSNBC Political Analyst Joy Reid, and

CNN Senior Political Correspondent Abby Phillip. There are many more, but these names will get you started. This is also a good time to curate whom you follow on social media. *Why should you follow a variety of Black women on social media?* Even if you're not particularly social media savvy, creating a Twitter or Facebook account and following Black women to hear our opinions on politics and current events will provide you with insight into issues important to the Black community. The key here is to follow a variety of people. The more voices you hear, the more well-rounded you'll become when discussing topics important to us.

The absence of Black female representation at the decision-making levels has dire consequences—especially on Black children. For example, Black women can address racial and educational disparities in schools by being elected to school boards. We know that very little Black history is taught. Instead, it falls to Black parents to fill that gap. Black people can change that by pressuring officials at the state and local levels to include our history in classroom curriculum. *Why do you think most schools teach very little Black history?* American history isn't simply white history. Black people have had an integral part in creating this country. Yet our importance is relegated to one month out of the year when we try to educate white people about our history. That tells me how little the people who decide student curriculum in this country care about Black history—and by extension, Black people. *How would integrating Black history into classroom curriculum help fight racism?*

Electing Black women to school boards also can help

protect Black children. A 2016 report by the Brookings Institution found that in U.S. schools, Black children were twice as likely to receive corporal punishment than white students. *How does that make you feel? Why do you think Black students are punished more?* The study found that, during the 2011–12 school year, 42,000 Black boys and 15,000 Black girls had been beaten. Black students were more likely to reside in states that extensively used corporal punishment. They also were more likely to receive this type of discipline. The majority of Black students beaten by teachers and administrators lived in the Deep South. The report stated that Black students in North Carolina and Georgia were "twice as likely to be struck as white students in North Carolina and Georgia, 70 percent more likely in Mississippi, 40 percent more likely in Louisiana, and 40 percent more likely in Arkansas." *How can allies help address this problem? What steps can you take?*

The researcher clarified that this disproportionate punishment of Black children didn't just happen in the South. In Pennsylvania and Michigan, Black children were also twice as likely to be hit. *Why is this problem not just in the South?* Black children in Maine were eight times as likely to be beaten than white children. In Colorado, Ohio, and California, the rate of corporal punishment for Black children was 70% higher than for white children. Black children were four times as likely as white children to receive in-school suspensions. Surprisingly, Wisconsin reported the highest rate of in-school suspensions for Black children. Washington, D.C., had the highest ratio of black-to-white suspensions.[21] *If Black students are punished more than white students in several states around the country, what are some of the beliefs of the ones meting out punishments?*

I used this study because of its stark examples of what happens when Black voices aren't heard. The disproportionate punishment of Black children in schools—which also includes arrests on campuses—creates a direct path for these children into the criminal justice system. This school-to-prison pipeline has been researched and debated for years. Black students face worse punishments than white students who commit the same infractions in school. *If you were a Black parent, how would you feel about this?* Consequently more Black students end up encountering law enforcement when police are called in to deal with their "infractions." There are many more examples of consequences when Black women aren't included in discussions and policies. That's why it's paramount that allies amplify our voices and pass the mic.

As an ally, you must help create spaces for Black women to speak. Recognize when you have the chance to pass the mic, then step aside. Too often, white voices drown out Black women to the point where we're silenced. We need allies to confront those situations and demand we're given a voice. Challenge yourself to look around and see where you can amplify our voices. Pass the mic every chance you get.

---

21   Startz, D. (2016, January 14). *Brown Center Chalkboard: Schools, black children, and corporal punishment.* Brookings. https://www.brookings.edu/blog/brown-center-chalkboard/2016/01/14/schools-black-children-and-corporal-punishment/

REINFORCE YOUR KNOWLEDGE

Use your journal to answer the following questions and discuss how you completed the actions.

Scenario

You're in a meeting with mostly white people. You notice that the two Black women in attendance are constantly interrupted and silenced by one of the white women in the meeting. Anytime they make a suggestion or ask a question, she either interrupts them or responds in a dismissive manner. What would you do to help the Black women? How would you handle the white woman?

Question 1: A Black woman is running for a city council seat. You've seen her at some local community meetings and want to help. How would you start? How would you persuade other white people to help with her campaign?

Question 2: How can you amplify the voices of Black women in other states? How can other allies help you?

Action

Make a list of at least five Black women you want to support. Think about political candidates, community leaders, racial justice leaders, business owners, etc. Figure out ways to assist them. Work with your racial justice group or accountability partner to identify them.

CONCLUSION

A long-term commitment

originally wanted to use this time to reinforce the main points I've covered in each chapter. Then Derek Chauvin was convicted for the murder of George Floyd. I'm still surprised at the outcome and shocked that this man will be punished for what he did when so many other police officers remain free. I want to talk about the guilty verdict and what it means to the Black community.

After generations of enduring racial violence, we finally got a small amount of justice. While we're happy Chauvin has been held accountable for his heinous act, nothing will ever bring Mr. Floyd back. His life mattered to so many people. I watched the press conference with his family. None of them were smiling. Of course, they were pleased with the verdict, but now they must try to heal from the trauma of losing him in such a violent and public way.

While his family continues to grieve, they will forever be remembered as the brothers, sisters, cousins, and uncles, of a man who died after a police officer forced the life from his body, even as George Floyd cried out for his mother. His family will always be a part of the public dialogue surrounding the systemic problem of police violence against Black people.

While Mr. Floyd's murderer was convicted, Breonna Taylor, Atatiana Jefferson, Tamir Rice, Freddie Gray, Sandra Bland, Philando Castile, and so many others died without any police officers held accountable for their deaths. *How did you feel about George Floyd's murder? What did others around you say? How would you begin educating white people about him and why he died?*

We don't have less work to do now. We have more. While there seems to be momentum gathering around police reform, it's easy for white people to think real change has happened because one officer was brought to justice. In fact, we have a long road ahead of us before we can say the tide has truly turned. Black people have always been beaten and murdered by police. Historically, law enforcement has treated Black people as animals to be hunted down and killed. The only reason the world is seeing the commonality of this practice is because of the ability to record it on a cell phone and distribute it worldwide via the Internet. Otherwise, more of white America would continue to believe Black people are exaggerating when we say the police aren't here to protect and serve us. They're another part of a system designed to keep us from achieving the equality we deserve. *How has your perception of the police and their relationship with Black people changed?* Your allyship is a lifelong commitment to anti-racism work. As an ally, every time you see a Black person stopped by police, that means you stop, too. You bear witness to that encounter. Record it. Make sure the officer knows you're there. Make it obvious that you're watching. Catch the eye of the Black person so they know someone is watching and that they're not alone. When I say use your white privilege for good, this is exactly what I mean. I've spoken to many white people who regularly stop to watch police encounters with Black people, and several have commented how officers toned down their behavior once they knew a white person was looking on. You might be asking if watching and filming encounters is safe for you. Generally, you have a First Amendment right to film police in public. According to NOLO.com, you just can't interfere with their duties. Having said that, you still must film and watch. It might be scary, but you also could save a Black life. **What concerns do you have about filming an encounter? How do you think watching and filming helps us fight racism?**

Now I want you to reflect on your journey so far. **What's been difficult? What surprised you? What has stood out to you?** Congratulate yourself for finishing the four weeks. Now it's time to buckle down and continue your anti-racism journey for the rest of your life. Allyship is like learning a new language. If you don't practice it, you'll lose all the new knowledge and skills you've worked so hard to attain. Remember you're in constant learning mode. Every day you're taking in information around you. Pay attention to what you see and hear. Now that you've begun to recognize racism and initiated conversations around the subject, you must keep performing those actions.

There's no gold medal for having a certain number of conversations with other white people. It's a lifelong endeavor. You'll never run out of white people to educate. Seek out the ones who are harmful to Black women and to the racial justice movement. Interject yourself into racist conversations and put your body—either virtually or physically—in between that white person and the Black woman on the receiving end of that violence. That's the work. That's how we create real change. *How have you prepared yourself for these confrontations? How will you get better at them?*

You now have other white people to help you. Use them regularly. This isn't work that can be done in a bubble. Take the time to listen to other allies tell their stories of educating and confronting racism and how they're fighting it both within themselves and in others. While you may never embrace being called a racist, it will happen. Take it in with a deep breath and listen. Then do the work to understand where you went wrong. Always make amends if you can. That apology should come with a deep understanding of the hurt you caused. You must clearly name the harm because we need to see that you understand your mistake. Write down every lesson you learn. Periodically go back and read them so you can better avoid those mistakes in the future. Remember, your experiences are some of the best tools you can use to teach other white people. Don't retreat from opening up about your own struggles. Tell those stories anytime you see that it might help someone else understand where they went wrong. While those stories might embarrass you, they will help others become more effective allies in this movement. Decenter your emotions. Instead, you should always center your efforts on uplifting and fighting for Black women. *Why should you share your mistakes with other white people doing ally work? Why should you also listen to their stories?*

Follow the lead of Black women every chance you get. You've joined a few racial justice groups. Broaden your perspective and look for groups that are addressing specific issues. Find organizations both in your community and online. Listen and learn from the Black women running them. You'll understand why that work is necessary and how those leaders are addressing racism. This will help you twofold: You'll help this organization through your allyship and activism, and you'll learn about that particular issue so you can explain it to others when the need arises. Your membership in these organizations gives you additional talking points when you're working with other white people. If you haven't followed multiple Black women on social media, start building that list. Ask other allies who they're following and why they chose them. Listen and learn from Black women and compensate us for their labor. Donate to our causes when you can and consistently amplify our voices. Remember that Black women aren't a monolith. So it's important to listen to different perspectives. This gives you the best chance of hearing a variety of opinions and experiences from us. Listening as we discuss the issues important to us will give you a deeper understanding of racial justice work and why there's such an urgent need to address these injustices. *What are a few things you've learned so far from Black women and other white people in your racial justice groups?*

Remember that discomfort allows you to grow as an ally. You must consciously push yourself out of your comfort zone to fight racism. You already know that the conversations you have with other white people won't always go as planned.

You'll continually encounter ones who refuse to change. However, don't make that decision after just one discussion with them. They've had a lifetime of believing their racist ideology. It takes multiple conversations with them for you to have any chance of changing their mind. Keep working on them. Challenge their racism and name it for them. You won't change every mind, but you can continually confront them. They should expect you to question their beliefs.

You must be the white person known for speaking up every single time. Nothing gets past you. You're the goalie, and racism is the hockey puck. Throw yourself in its path and slap it away. You want to be the family member known to speak your mind about racism and who refuses to give anyone a pass—not your coworkers, family, or friends. That's the reputation of an effective ally. Sometimes a simple "What did you say?" is all that's needed to stop a racist in their tracks and begin their education. Use your past discomfort during encounters with other white people to stay focused when this conversation gets uncomfortable. If you're too comfortable, you need to engage on a deeper level that allows you to learn and grow. *Why should you step outside your comfort zone and not become complacent?*

Recognize that, while discomfort leads to growth, defensiveness leads to stagnation. You'll become defensive at times. You can't avoid it. However, you can learn how to manage your reactions. Don't make excuses for your mistakes. Don't refuse to listen. Don't walk away from the conversation. Listen to what the other person is saying and find the truth in their words. Check in with other allies so you can better understand what happened. Anytime you exhibit defensiveness when you're confronted on actions you took or words you said—and you *will be* confronted—you stop learning the real lessons needed to fight for Black women. Always keep that goal in mind—you're here to fight for us. You can and will feel defensive, but work through it and keep going. Communicate those feelings with other allies so you can learn from that defensiveness. ***How can you work through those feelings? What are some tools you can use?***

Acknowledging you benefit from white privilege goes a long way toward becoming an ally we can depend on to fight with us. If you refuse to believe that white privilege exists, it's impossible for you to effectively confront racism. White privilege is wrapped up in racism and white supremacy. It doesn't exist without the other two. Yes, you benefit from it. You receive unfair advantages just because of the color of your skin. In April 2021, another Black man was murdered by police. Daunte Wright was shot to death by Kim Potter, a 26-year veteran officer, who claims she mistook her gun for her taser. On December 23, 2021, she was convicted of first- and second-degree manslaughter. I know Black men and women who have been stopped by the police multiple times. Many were handcuffed and placed in the back of the police car because they fit the description of a suspect, or they had a taillight out, or . . . the police just felt like stopping them. Obviously, white people get pulled over, too, but the difference is Black people are afraid of not making it out of the encounter alive, even if they do everything right.

That's white privilege. Generally, you have positive

experiences with the police. You're not regularly seeing new hashtags of white people who have lost their lives for no reason other than they're white. You're not watching as most of these officers go unpunished. If you won't acknowledge that your skin color gives you privilege over us, you'll never be the type of ally we look to when we need help. Instead, when your ally work gets too hard, you'll retreat into that white privilege and abandon your anti-racism stance. You can't use your privilege for good if you're lying to yourself about its existence. *How can your white privilege help you in anti-racism work? How have you seen that privilege benefit you?*

We know that white men wield the most power in this country and white women enjoy their adjacency to that power. White men must acknowledge their unfair advantages, but white women must stop supporting white supremacy by protecting their status of loyally standing by their men. White women also have used their white womanhood so that white men believe they need protecting and defending. They've used it as a weapon against Black people as they join forces with white men to control us. It's time for white women to hold themselves accountable for the way they also use the police to oppress us. Their desire to keep white supremacist systems in place is how their racism shows itself. White women must make the decision to step away from their adjacency to white male power and decide they want to stand in their own beliefs and support racial equality. That means fighting for Black women and against white supremacy and racism. They also must acknowledge their complicity in white supremacy and commit to using their power for the good of the fight. *How do*

white women harm themselves and anti-racism work when
they choose to stay power-adjacent to white men?

Throughout this book, I emphasize that allies take action. Don't get stuck in the theory of racism. Yes, you must constantly educate yourself about the past, but that will never replace taking the necessary steps of confronting racism. You can read every book about racism on the market. However, if you never take those lessons and apply them to real life, you're merely collecting information. We don't need white people in this movement who have convinced themselves education on its own changes anything. These white people believe that learning about racism through books and documentaries or joining an anti-racism group and reading along while allies talk about their experiences doing the work means they're allies, too.

How are you an ally if you're not willing to confront racism, even in yourself? Your lack of action means you're allowing racism to flourish around you *and* within you, and you refuse to stop it. Even though this book gives you a solid foundation to begin ally work, if you simply read it and never act on what you've learned, you haven't joined the anti-racism movement. You're not fighting for me and other Black women. Ask yourself why you've stopped short of transitioning from words to actions. Are you scared? If so, work through that fear with an accountability partner or in your affinity group. Bring it up with other white people in your racial justice group. You took the time to read this book. Take the needed time to learn what it means to do anti-racism work. You won't convince anyone of your commitment if all you can do is quote books written by and about Black people. ***What scares you about this work? How will you work through those fears?***

You've probably heard this African proverb: "Each one, teach one." It arose during the time when enslaved Africans in the United States were denied a formal education. So it became the responsibility of any African who learned to read or write to teach others. Remember this proverb as you're learning about racism and educating other white people. You should regularly discuss the knowledge you've gained and impart that wisdom on other white people who can benefit from it. This is the information you give to white people you want to influence so they can learn about how their racism affects Black women. Focus on your inner circle. Pay attention to your family and friends. Listen to what other white people say at work. Be prepared to confront them by questioning their beliefs and following it up with information. Educating people you love can be your most difficult work. Your emotions will run high, and their words and actions will affect you on a more intimate level. You might endure personal attacks and racial slurs aimed at you because of your stance. At some point, you must decide if having them in your life is more important than your anti-racist beliefs. However, if you keep them in your life, commit to regularly confronting them about their racism. You can't pick and choose when you want to do the work. Allies never let racism slide. ***How will you stay focused on the work when confronting family and friends?***

If you're friends with a Black woman, don't ask her to educate you about racism. If you really care about her, you'll let her know you're committed to the racial justice fight for the equality of all Black women. You don't need to ask her what you can do. That information is readily available to you through other white people also working to become anti-racists. Let her know you're available if she ever needs to talk. If she chooses to open up to you, don't question her experiences. If you do, you'll lose that connection and perhaps even the friendship. I wrote this book because I want white people to learn from each other and listen to Black women. Plenty of us hold workshops and lectures about racism. Many of us run anti-racism groups and other organizations geared toward fighting racial inequality. There's no reason you should burden your Black friend with educating you. If she offers to discuss racism with you, be grateful for her labor and compensate her in some way. Never assume you deserve a free education about racism from her or any other Black woman. *How would you handle seeing a white person demanding Black women educate her? What resources would you use and how would you begin the discussion?*

You must keep learning, but your journey should always center Black women. Your commitment to us shouldn't change. We're not looking for an entourage of white people to make us feel good. We want allies willing to fight against racism and white supremacy. You'll have successes and failures at this goal. In fact, you'll have more of the latter. Too many white people refuse to change, but that doesn't mean you quit. When you have successes, celebrate them but also learn from them. Don't become addicted to compliments from others when you've succeeded. Once you focus on hearing accolades, you become a performative ally. You'll do what's necessary to receive praise. You'll convince yourself that you're still doing the work. Otherwise, why are people cheering you? **What is the danger in becoming a performative ally?**

Remember what I said about ranking yourself against other white people. Striving to become the wokest white person only makes you a fake ally. We can't depend on you to keep learning about yourself and to strive not to harm Black women. As soon as you choose the performative path, the idea of educating other white people goes out the window. You're too busy seeing who's watching as you demean and abuse other allies. While that might feel good in the moment, you don't help us gain any ground with this behavior. Allies will screw up. If you're performing for others, you're forgetting this important lesson. You're not using what you've learned, and that makes you more dangerous to us than a new ally who's open to understanding the work they need to do and stepping into uncomfortable situations. Check in with yourself to make sure you're doing anti-racism work for the right reasons. **How will you refocus when you find yourself becoming performative?**

Remember to pass the mic. Black women have our own stories to share. We have expertise we want to monetize. We have knowledge we want to impart onto others. Oftentimes, white people hold the key to opening the door into spaces we're rarely allowed. Commit yourself to inviting us into those places where you see few of us represented amongst your ranks. Challenge your organizations about why we're not there. We want the same opportunities as you to succeed, and we need allies to help us get there. Make a way for us to speak every chance you get. Whether it's at a protest or in the boardroom, make space for us to have a voice. We add value through our unique opinions and experiences. We just need the chance to share them. *How can you pass the mic today?*

This handbook should have been an arduous journey of self-discovery and education for you. Take some time to reflect on the experience. Reread your journal to see your progress over these four weeks. Discuss any questions you have with your accountability partner or affinity group. Check in with others in your racial justice group. Now is the time to get answers so you have a solid base to continue. As you're reading your journal, think about what you can share with others. Remember that you always should be considering who can benefit from your experiences and what you've learned on this journey.

The information you've obtained will help you to become a more effective ally, but you'll never be perfect. Your work in this arena is neverending. Allyship is a lifetime commitment. Racism and white supremacy permeate every aspect of society. We would be kidding ourselves if we thought we could fix everything in a short period of time. We're in this for the long haul, and we need allies to work with us for the rest of their lives. That way, they become better at the work and have more wisdom to share with other white people. That's the work. It's grueling. It's hard. It's frustrating.

But that's how you set Black women free.

ONGOING QUESTIONS EVERY ALLY SHOULD REGULARLY CONSIDER WHEN DOING ANTI-RACIST WORK:

How will you keep learning?

How will you pursue discomfort
on your journey?

How will you confront racism everywhere?

How will you educate the ones you love?

How will you stay focused
on anti-racism work?

How will you center, uplift,
and fight for Black women?

How will you stay committed
to a lifetime journey as an ally?

THE WHITE ALLIES HANDBOOK

. . . .

Lecia Michelle

ABOUT THIS GUIDE

These additional questions and materials will enhance your group's reading of Lecia Michelle's *The White Allies Handbook*.

FURTHER READING

Alexander, M. (2020). *The new Jim Crow: Mass incarceration in the age of colorblindness*. (10th Anniversary Edition). The New Press.

Anderson, C. (2016). *White rage: The unspoken truth of our racial divide*. Bloomsbury USA.

Baldwin, J. (1992). *The fire next time*. Vintage.

Coates, T. (2015). *Between the world and me*. One World.

Cobbina, J. (2019). *Hands up, don't shoot: Why the protests in Ferguson and Baltimore matter, and how they changed America*. NYU Press.

Cooper, B. (2018). *Eloquent rage: A Black feminist discovers her superpower*. St. Martin's Press.

Davis, A. Y. (1983). *Women, race and class*. Vintage.

Drake, H. L. (2019). *Dear white women, it's not you. It's me. I'm breaking up with you*. Drake Publishing.

Du Bois, W. E. B. (2016). *The souls of black folk*. (Dover Thrift Editions. Unabridged). Dover Publications.

Fleming, C. M. (2019). *How to be less stupid about race: On racism, white supremacy and the racial divide*. Beacon Press.

Franklin, J. H. (2010). *From slavery to freedom: A history of African Americans*. McGraw-Hill.

Hartman, S. (2019). *Wayward lives, beautiful experiments: Intimate histories of social upheaval*. W. W. Norton & Company.

Hill, D. B. (2019). *A bound woman is a dangerous thing: The incarceration of African American women from Harriet Tubman to Sandra Bland*. Bloomsbury Publishing.

Hooks, B. (2014). *Ain't I a woman: Black women and feminism.* Routledge.

Ifill, S. A. (2018). *On the courthouse lawn, revised edition: Confronting the legacy of lynching in the twenty-first century.* Beacon Press.

Jones-Rogers, S. E. (2019). *They were her property.* Yale University Press.

Joseph, P. E. (2020). *The sword and the shield: The revolutionary lives of Malcolm X and Dr. Martin Luther King, Jr.* Basic Books.

Khan-Cullors, P. & bandele, a. (2018). *When they call you a terrorist: A Black Lives Matter memoir.* St. Martin's Press.

Lorde, A. (2007). *Sister outsider: Essays and speeches.* Crossing Press.

Lowery, W. (2017). *They can't kill us all: The story of Black Lives Matter.* PENGUIN GROUP.

Muhammad, K.G. (2010). *The condemnation of blackness: Race, crime and the making of modern urban America.* Harvard University Press.

Oluo, I. (2019). *So you want to talk about race.* Seal Press.

Rothstein, R. (2017). *The color of law: A forgotten history of how our government segregated America.* Liveright.

Taylor, K. Y. (2019). *Race for profit: How banks and the real estate industry undermined Black homeownership.* The University of North Carolina Press.

Washington, H. A. (2006). *Medical apartheid: The dark history of medical experimentation on Black Americans from colonial times to the present.* Doubleday.

Wilder, C. S. (2013). *Ebony and ivory: Race, slavery, and the troubled history of America's universities.* Bloomsbury Publishing.

Wilkerson, I. (2011). *The warmth of other suns: The epic story of America's Great Migration.* Vintage.

Wilson, M. & Russell, K. (1995). *Divided sisters: Bridging the gap between black women & white women.* Doubleday.

PLACES TO VISIT

The Africa Center (New York City, NY):
https://www.theafricacenter.org/

African-American Panoramic Experience (Atlanta, GA):
https://www.apexmuseum.org/

Harriet Tubman Museum of Cape May (Cape May, NJ):
https://www.harriettubmanmuseum.org/

The Legacy Museum (Montgomery, AL):
https://museumandmemorial.eji.org/

Martin Luther King, Jr., National Historic Site (Atlanta, GA):
https://www.nps.gov/malu/index.htm

Mary McLeod Bethune Council House (Washington, D.C.):
https://www.nps.gov/mamc/index.htm

Museum for Black Girls (Denver, CO):
https://www.themuseumforblackgirls.com/

Museum of African American History (Boston, MA):
https://www.maah.org/

Museum of African Diaspora (San Francisco, CA):
https://www.moadsf.org/

The National Center for Civil and Human Rights (Atlanta, GA):
https://www.civilandhumanrights.org/

National Museum of African American History & Culture
(Washington, D.C.): https://nmaahc.si.edu/

PLACES TO VISIT

National Museum of African American Music (Nashville, TN):
    https://nmaam.org/

The National Voting Rights Museum and Institute (Selma, AL):
    http://nvrmi.com/

Omenala Griot Afrocentric Museum (Atlanta, GA):
    http://www.omenalagriot.com/

The Whitney Plantation (Edgard, LA):
    https://www.whitneyplantation.org/

DISCUSSION QUESTIONS

1. How has your own upbringing influenced your thoughts about race? Growing up, who had the most influence over you? What would you change about your childhood so you better understood racism?

2. Which issues surrounding racism are most pressing to you? How will you support the efforts of Black women fighting those issues? How will you find other allies to join you?

3. Why is becoming an ally to Black women difficult for many white people? What obstacles do they face that could derail their journey?

4. Why are authentic conversations in any friendship important? How does it benefit each person in that relationship? What skills can you develop to help you become a better friend to Black women?

5. How can you work with other allies to address racial justice without centering yourself? Why is centering yourself a common problem with white allies?

6. What are some ways you can address racism? How would you begin the conversation? What resources could you use to educate another white person?

7. What will stop you from quitting when you tire of doing anti-racist work? How will you use other allies to stay the course? What can you say to another person who is considering quitting?

8. Why is it important to be anti-racist? What is the difference between anti-racist and "not racist"?

9. You can support Black women by passing the mic. What does passing the mic mean to you? Why is this an important part of racial justice work? How does it benefit Black women?

10. How can you prevent yourself from becoming a performative ally? How would you address someone who is exhibiting performative behavior? What are the effects of performative allyship on racial justice work?

11. What have you learned about your own racism? Why should you constantly be aware of that racism when doing anti-racist work? What happens if you don't acknowledge it?

12. How would you help someone new to allyship work on their defensiveness? What stories about your own challenges would you tell? How would you explain the harm caused by defending racist words and actions?

13. How does white privilege factor into ally work? Why should white people acknowledge they benefit from it? How can they use it to fight racism?

14. What would you do if another white person called you a performative ally? What questions would you ask to find out? How can you use other allies to help? How would you work on your performative behavior?

15. Why is it important not to objectify the Black people in your life? For example, what is the problem with responding that you're a white person with a Black spouse when you're confronted about your racist behavior?

16. What happens if you decide you've learned enough as an ally? How does that affect your work? Why is it important to keep learning?

17. How will you address racism amongst your family and friends? What is one way to start the conversation? How will you feel if that person you love decides they won't change? How would your relationship with them change?